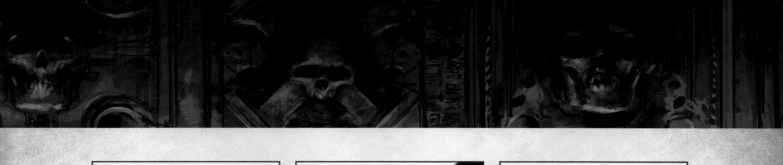

GREY KNIGHTS

BY THE WILL OF THESE FEW IS MANKIND SHIELDED FROM TRUE
DARKNESS. THEY WIELD THE SECRET FIRE THAT PURIFIES CORRUPTION.
THEIR MINDS ARE BARRED AGAINST PRIDE, ARMED AGAINST DIABOLIC
DECEPTION. WITH ANOINTED BLADES THEY BANISH INFERNAL
NIGHTMARES MADE FLESH. THEY ARE THE EMPEROR'S FINAL BOON TO
HUMANITY – A GIFT MANKIND WILL NEVER BE ALLOWED TO FATHOM.

CONTENTS

PRODUCED BY THE WARHAMMER STUDIO

With thanks to the Mournival and the Infinity Circuit for their additional playtesting services

Codex: Grey Knights © Copyright Games Workshop Limited 2021. Codex: Grey Knights, GW, Games Workshop, Space Marine, 40K, Warhammer, Warhammer 40,000, the 'Aquila' Double-headed Eagle logo, and all associated logos, illustrations, images, names, creatures, races, vehicles, locations, weapons, characters, and the distinctive likenesses thereof, are either ® or TM, and/or © Games Workshop Limited, variably registered around the world. All Rights Reserved.

No part of this publication may be reproduced, stored in a retrieval system, or transmitted in any form or by any means, electronic, mechanical, photocopying, recording or otherwise, without the prior permission of the publishers.

This is a work of fiction. All the characters and events portrayed in this book are fictional, and any resemblance to real people or incidents is purely coincidental. British Cataloguing-in-Publication Data. A catalogue record for this book is available from the British Library. Pictures used for illustrative purposes only.

Certain Citadel products may be dangerous if used incorrectly and Games Workshop does not recommend them for use by children under the age of 16 without adult supervision. Whatever your age, be careful when using glues, bladed equipment and sprays and make sure that you read and follow the instructions on the packaging.

Games Workshop Ltd, Willow Rd, Lenton, Nottingham, NG7 2WS
games-workshop.com

INTRODUCTION

Fear the daemon no longer, for herein lies the secrets to its banishment! Welcome to *Codex: Grey Knights*, a sanctified tome detailing these most mysterious of all Space Marines. Within these pages, you will discover the brotherhoods of these daemon-hunting psychic warriors, examples of their noble heraldries and all the rules needed to wield an army of them in battle.

The Grey Knights are the most elite Chapter of the Adeptus Astartes. Forged in secret ten thousand years ago, they form Humanity's greatest weapon against its direst threat: daemons, murderous sentiences squeezed from the stuff of Chaos. In the Grey Knights' sequestered fortress on the moon of Titan, omens of daemonic incursions are sifted from the warp. With this foreknowledge, they despatch strike forces of daemon-hunting Space Marines, battle tanks and hulking combat walkers. Each genetically enhanced warrior wears sigil-wrought armour that wards against the warp energies of their prey. They wield arcane blades and hammers, as anathema to the otherworldly flesh of daemons as to the mortal frames of the malfeasant, the deluded or the merely ignorant. A Grey Knight's greatest weapon, however, is his mind, for with it he resists corruption and blasts his foes with empyric fire.

Grey Knights offer established players and newcomers to the hobby alike the chance to field a potent combination of post-human might and sanctified psychic assaults on the tabletop. They represent some of the most powerful units in the Warhammer 40,000 game; as an elite faction, even a small number of models make for an incredibly formidable force. With volleys of blistering firepower, a raft of potent psychic powers and unique empyric weaponry, your Grey Knights will cut down swathes of lighter foes, out-think and outmanoeuvre your enemy's force and topple the deadliest units your opponent can throw at them. Powerful battle tanks provide mobile bastions for your force as agile gunships and warp-shunting Interceptors outflank your opponent's warriors. All the while, your teleport strikes allow the capture of distant and vital objectives.

There are few more stirring sights than an entire army of Grey Knights. Each model's armour is covered in the ornate iconography of the Chapter, allowing painters to lavish all kinds of details onto them. Conversely, they can also be incredibly simple to paint; their detailed surfaces and metallic armour mean just simple techniques can be used to make them stand out. With little effort, a Battle Ready force can be quickly assembled and look glorious facing down their enemies.

This Codex contains all the background, rules and inspiring photos of painted models you need to collect your own strike force of Grey Knights. Within these pages, you will also discover a wealth of evocative Crusade content that adds extra layers of depth to your games, as your Grey Knights continue their endless war to banish daemonkind and crush those who consort with the Ruinous Powers.

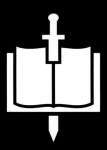

Humanity is beset by countless evils. Against many, armies can be raised, hatred can be stoked, vigilance for that which is not Human can be maintained. Not so the daemon, the lie made flesh, for to even know of such creatures is to risk one's essence.

The soul of the Grey Knights is sacrosanct, and their purity is incorruptible. The silvered armour of this Chapter's warriors is bound with incantations, engraved with sigils of warding. Their blades shine with the inner light of their sanctity, for each of these Space Marines is a psychic warrior, in empyric communion with his battle-brothers. Empowered by minds constantly on guard, they can cut steel with bare hands, their eyes blaze with fire and even the power of their words flays the otherworldly skin of daemons.

In shadow do these Knights of Titan fight — from the underbelly of teeming worlds full of mortal pawns, to mutating planets slick with the taint of the empyrean, where lesser warriors' sanity would not survive. They are the Imperium's surest defence against that which the Emperor foresaw would be its greatest threat. The Grey Knights are Humanity's blade against the daemon, and only they offer Mankind hope of anything more than hollow victories.

There are those who might see contradiction between our abhorrence of the daemon and our wielding of sorcery. Yet these contradictions live only in the minds of weak men, and we are not accountable to such as they.

THE 666TH CHAPTER

None now alive can claim to know the origins of the Grey Knights with certainty. The Chapter themselves have a single written account of their founding, housed in their fortress monastery – the Citadel of Titan. From this and other legendary sources known to very few, a story of dire peril, a priceless gift and the concealment of soul-shattering knowledge can be pieced together.

It was during the final days of the Horus Heresy, so it is said, that the founders of the Grey Knights were first convened. Even as the Emperor, his generals and advisors prepared Terra for the onslaught of his wayward son, the Arch-traitor Horus, the Master of Mankind contemplated threats even greater. Certain myths of that distant age hint that the Emperor alone foresaw the danger posed by Chaos and the immaterium's denizens: its daemons and gods. These coalescences of emotion, given terrible existence in the warp, would not be satisfied by Mankind's destruction, only by its corruption, subjugation and eternal torment. Ambiguous references suggest the Emperor's most trusted servant, Malcador the Sigillite, scoured the war-torn Imperium while the Heresy raged, directed by the Emperor to seek individuals whose shoulders would bear the burden of saving Humanity's future.

Among those Malcador eventually presented to the Emperor, it is thought that there were eight Space Marines. Peerless in their dedication to the Imperium, aware of the warp's threat and potent in their esoteric abilities, each of the eight were approved and the Emperor tasked Malcador with the next stage.

REFUND AND RETURN

Malcador took the group of Space Marines to Titan, a frigid moon of Saturn. Through means now unknown, the Sigillite had hidden the Emperor's works on Titan from traitors and loyalists alike. According to one electro-tapestry, Malcador revealed a fortress monastery, established in desperate secrecy. Inside it were the means to found a Chapter – one not descended from the Legions that still fought, but forged anew with gene-seed wrought by the Emperor in isolation. How long it had taken such a plan to unfold, how long it had taken to find suitable recruits, forge specialist weapons and wargear, and more besides, perhaps not even Malcador knew. It is suspected that it was he who appointed one of the eight, known to legend as Janus, to lead the nascent Chapter as its first Supreme Grand Master.

What happened next has slipped even from the true understanding of the Grey Knights. With Terra herself braced to face the heretical Legions of Horus, a sorcerous enchantment of unprecedented power loosened Titan from reality's grip. The moon vanished from its orbit, sliding into the warp. Time and bloodshed overtook the Sol System. Titan endured, anchored somehow in the empyrean. Those upon it, unaware of the Heresy's tragic conclusion, toiled to bring the Emperor's gift to Humanity to fruition while titanic energies strove to protect the world from the warp's roiling embrace.

Years passed in realspace – and who knows how many within the timeless warp – before Titan reappeared. When it did so, it was during the confusion and anarchy of the Second Founding. The growing Inquisition, it is whispered, had a hand in much of that endeavour's work. It is in records of the Second Founding that the Grey Knights first appear, enshrined as the 666th Chapter of the Adeptus Astartes.

THE SECRET WAR

The warriors those Inquisitors found – a thousand in number, they were told, and neophytes no longer – were ready to enact the Emperor's intent immediately. With their allies in the Inquisition helping to keep secret their existence, the Grey Knights began their hidden war. As a fighting force, only they could face the daemon without fear of taint. The existence of such beings, and the sorcery used to banish them, must forever remain unknown, all witnesses expunged.

THE ORDO MALLEUS

Some say that when Malcador presented to the Emperor his exceptional individuals, besides the Space Marines there were shadowy men and women of steely and enquiring nature. The truly incautious suggest the Inquisition itself had its origins in the same conclave.

The Ordo Malleus is one of the primary organs of that feared institution. Its diverse members investigate traces of Chaos, the daemonic and anything tainted by the warp. Nowhere and no one is beneath or beyond their gimlet gaze. To root out solitary miners tainted by long-buried artefacts, mutant bordellos among heaving hive cities weakening the warp's barriers with

debaucheries, even daemonic possession of those at the highest levels, an Inquisitor has near-limitless power and no qualms about its application.

Ordo Malleus Inquisitors are iron-willed individuals, granted access to knowledge of Chaos that would drive lesser people insane. Though they employ vast resources, and requisition almost any forces they see fit, they work most closely with the Grey Knights. When extensive daemonic presences are exposed, often only the brothers of Titan can exorcise it. The two bodies often share information, yet maintain a wary eye on each other in a complex and oft-strained rapport.

TITAN

Titan's frozen landscape of cryovolcanoes and oceans of liquid methane is broken by jagged spurs of black rock. It is a grim and forbidding place that barely supports basic life. Such barrenness is but one of the veils that shrouds its warriors.

Should a ship be allowed anywhere near the surface of Titan, it will already have passed barriers and guards of many kinds. The ship's sensors may have noticed some, such as unusual vessels circling in the dark suggested by ghost returns. Those aboard with strange technologies or esoteric powers may feel proud in their detection of yet others: lattices of power that fish for interdimensional prey, or unsleeping stations housing psychic choirs that sing the forts' existences out of people's minds. There are far more layers of diversion, obfuscation and extermination that rival – and in certain ways exceed – those around Terra itself, down to Titan's seemingly lifeless surface.

Jutting from the ice sheets in the shadow of Mount Anarch, the Citadel of Titan has endured since its raising in a time of legend. It is the fortress monastery of the Grey Knights and among its black, basalt spires are emplaced batteries of macro cannons and defence lasers. Inside the Citadel of Titan's unwelcoming exterior, dusty passages and cavernous halls echo merely to the sweep of robes and the scratch of mnemo-quills. Though designed to house an entire Chapter and all the arms and vehicles, serfs and servitors they require, many are the arming chambers, meditation cells and feast halls that lie empty for years. Distance is no obstacle to the daemonic threat, and in opposing that threat most Grey Knights are scattered, fighting among the stars while the Citadel of Titan awaits their victorious return.

Great walls and columns are engraved with the Grey Knights' battle honours, and grand banners and trophies are hung in the Hall of Champions. In the fortress' depths lie the Chambers of Purity, said to guard – among other horrors – the most sacred or dangerous relics that the Grey Knights recover. Yet the Sons of Titan could not win so many victories were it not for their foresight.

THE AUGURIUM

Atop the fortress monastery's highest black spire is a single, silver pinnacle: the Augurium. Within the mirrored walls of its vaulted chambers, the Prognosticars of the Grey Knights sift through their reflected thoughts and dowse the shifting strands of timeless probabilities from the warp. Prognosticars are powerful psykers who, among guttering candles and drifts of incense, read psychic tremors and fluctuations to divine the location and time of daemonic incursions.

Nothing connected with the warp is entirely accurate or safe, but via the Prognosticars' careful unpicking of lies, the spoor of the daemon can be traced. With the visions and wisdom of the Prognosticars, the Grey Knights can even be in place before an incursion occurs, rather than wait for the planet's panicked astropathic plea, by which time it is often too late. The Grey Knights anticipate and prepare like no other force of the Imperium, knowing in advance the nature of the threat they face and perhaps something of the consequences of failure.

SANCTUM SANCTORUM

Secure as only the spiritual heart of the Grey Knights could be, this vast shielded chamber and its countless connected vaults, halls and alcoves contain the accumulated lore of the Chapter. The Sanctum Sanctorum's towering shelves of tomes, crumbling scrolls, data-crystals and info-wafers hold the Chapter's forbidden knowledge. The names of proscribed cults and doomed xenos races can be found here alongside the forge-secrets of Nemesis force weapons. Details of the Chapter's psychic ceremonies and communions, set down on stone tablets, holo-discs or stranger media, shelter in stasis vaults, and in frozen, truesilvered crypts rest the Chapter's genetic legacies.

THE WARP NEXUS

A star-shaped chamber at the heart of the Citadel of Titan resounds to the ceaseless chants and prayers of hundreds of Chapter serfs. This is the Warp Nexus. It is written that the hexagrammic sigils and graven designs therein protected Titan and its fortress monastery during their years within the warp, and were even the means of its transition between realms. It is maintained as a tangible artefact – supposedly left by Malcador the Sigillite – but also in the hope that it may once again grant an extreme refuge if needed.

THE TERMINUS DECREE

Deep within the Chambers of Purity, locked away in the hall said to hold the tomb of the Sigillite himself, rests a simple wooden box, embellished with a golden seal. Within this box, written upon ancient parchment, is the instruction known only as the Terminus Decree. This artefact goes unrecorded in the libraries of the Imperium, for it is kept secret from all but the Supreme Grand Master of the Grey Knights.

Only the Supreme Grand Master knows how to open the box, and he will do so only when all hope for the future of Humanity seems lost. The Terminus Decree is the ultimate sanction of the Grey Knights, a secret so vast it could bring the Imperium to its knees, or save it in its darkest hour.

The exact nature of the document is unknown, for no one has ever opened it, and the only clue to its contents lies in the box's golden seal. It is whispered that it is the exact match of another seal, found only at one sacred spot in all the Imperium's many scattered worlds: the Emperor's Golden Throne.

The deadly infinitudes of existence are myriad. The twisted forms of the daemon. The sibilant lies of the daemon. The profane works of the daemon. The miserable thralls of the daemon. And the extent

ET TEMPLARS MYSTERIA
AUX ORDO MALLEUS

Praise the Emperor for His sacrifice,
as He endures so shall we.
We who are Hunters of Daemons,
shall strive in his name eternally.

We His order of soul-wards,
shall delve into the Dark Shadows.
We shall seek out the Tainted,
we shall pursue the Vilest Evil.

It is we who stand guard,
our Eternal Watch shall not fail.
For we are the Brethren Incorruptis!

We Grey Knights are the Hammers,
we slay the Darkness without fear.
Founded in great mystery we were,
Chapter six hundred and sixty six.

Though on Titan we be hidden,
yet our eyes encompass the Galaxy.
No Helspawn shall elude our gaze,
no daemon shall avoid its Fate.

We shall be the Keepers Immortal,
all Secrets shall be our Knowledge.
We are the Guardians of Mankind!

Caution and secrecy are our code,
watchfulness and patience are our way.
Hidden from the Eyes of Chaos,
we strike without warning or dread.

Though we find ourselves in Shadows,
no Blackness will enter our Hearts.
No treachery will touch our souls,
no pride will sully our thoughts.

We shall be Pure amongst Impurity,
we shall be Innocence amongst Guilt.
We are the Imperium's Hidden Saviours!

We are spread across the Heavens,
our watch is untiring and ceaseless.
The Emperor shall guard our Souls,
as we Guard those of others.

Our will shall be our weapons,
our faith shall be our armour.
Our minds will be secure fortresses,
no Temptation will weaken our resolve.

Though unnumbered lurking perils await us,
our blades will ever be ready.
For we are the Emperor's Vengeance!

Masters of all weapons are we,
no defence exists against our wrath.
With the Nemesis shall we fight,
with an Aegis to shield us.

In bloodshed shall we save Mankind,
Death shall be our Everlasting Creed.
War Unending shall be our Fate,
in battle shall we be steeped.

We shall be unstinting in Hatred,
we shall hunger for Holy War.
For we are Swords of Justice!

When all flee in hideous disarray,
strong and sound shall we stand.
Cowardice is wholly unknown to us,
our courage comes from the Emperor.

Unbowed and unshaken against all foes,
we shall claim victory with blood.
Steady and surely we hunt them,
those that dare oppose our wrath.

Death stalks us in many forms,
the grotesque and the utterly inhuman.
We are the Bringers of Hope!

Bloody battles unending constantly await us,
redemption the reward for our vigilance.
When Possession rears its unspeakable head,
ours is the blade that descends.

When Empyrean Horrors invade our realm,
our Exorcisms shall hurl them back.
There is no Chaos spawned horror,
which can resist our indomitable anger.

With undaunted courage we shall prevail,
no arcane magicks shall overcome us.
We are the Bearers of Victory!

No corruption shall blemish our Galaxy,
no Immaterial Fiend shall be spared.
No Malevolent Spirit will oppose us,
no Creation of Sin shall survive.

No Unholy Deed shall go Unpunished,
all Blasphemous Acts shall be Atoned.
No Spawn of Misrule avoids us,
all are banished to the Void.

Nothing shall evade our Cleansing Fire,
not daemon or Spawn or Renegade.
For we are Mankind's Divine Blade!

Emperor's Blessings are laid upon us,
the Warp is ours to Tame.
Though Sorceries shall be against us,
no Witchcraft will bring our Doom.

Though Spell or Incantation blocks us,
the Emperor shall see us Victorious.
No Hex can overcome our determination,
our resolve is strong as steel.

Sigils and wards watch over us,
prayers shall serve as our Guide.
For we are the Emperor's Chosen!

There is much darkness awaiting us,
yet the Emperor lights our path.
Falsehood surrounds us at every turn,
yet no Traitor shall confound us.

No despicable trickery will thwart us,
no Damnation shall bring us low.
There is no peace for us,
for an eternity we will strive.

Though mere mortals in His service,
everlasting shall be our True Duty.
Et Imperator Invocato Diabolus
Daemonica Exorcism!

The Canticle of Absolution of the Grey Knights, known as The Six Hundred and Sixty-six Secret Words.
Quaternary source: corrupted datafile O/223/Inq\6a:: Excrucio validation pending + + +

DAEMON HUNTING

Daemons are not creatures of flesh and blood. They are beings of the darkest myth and madness. To hunt and battle such monsters requires embracing that madness and wielding it as a weapon, fighting sorcery with sorcery. No ordinary Human psyker could do so without risking their mind becoming a yawning portal for the daemons of Chaos to pour through. Grey Knights are trained to channel their sanctified powers into a halo of protective wards known as the Aegis. Emanating from each Grey Knight's soul, it weaves through enchanted sigils and silver circuitry in his armour, radiating as a nimbus of purity that makes his presence anathema to daemonkind. So armoured, Grey Knights can withstand the forbidden powers they must employ to destroy the daemon.

The Grey Knights have access to weapons that fire ritually engraved bolts, and they wield force weapons that act as energised conduits for the wielder's own psychic power. Such arms can damage or destroy the quasi-physical shell a daemon inhabits once manifested. Chief among the Grey Knights' strategies for vanquishing a daemon, however, is the knowing of the beast's True Name. Such knowledge grants great power, which is why daemons adopt misleading titles and why Grey Knights relinquish their birth names upon induction to the Chapter. To a Grey Knight, a True Name is as reliable a weapon as his storm bolter. A freshly ordained Grey Knight can invoke a True Name at a moment's notice to disorient and weaken his foe, while some veterans can employ one to destroy the daemon's physical form, or even banish it back into the warp. These are not lasting victories, for within the warp a daemon may eventually regather its essence and coalesce around its hatred of he who banished it.

In their endless war against those that cannot truly be killed, a Grey Knight faces annihilation at every turn. It is the fervent wish of every battle-brother that upon his death he be carried back to Titan to be interred in the consecrated crypts of the Dead Fields. These catacombs have accepted the honoured dead of the Chapter since its earliest days. The warrior's body is ritually cleansed and the six hundred and sixty-six words of sanctity are inscribed upon his skin before he is laid to rest with honour and solemnity.

CHAPTER ORGANISATION

Though recorded as a Second Founding Chapter, the Grey Knights do not follow the Codex Astartes: the great work whose edicts underpinned the creation of those brotherhoods. Instead, the secretive Grey Knights follow the tenets of structure they believe were handed down by Malcador the Sigillite, tenets born of the unique demands of their war against the Dark Gods.

The Grey Knights maintain a strength of approximately a thousand battle-brothers. This does not include officers or specialists and, like all Space Marine Chapters, the small army of mostly mortal serfs and cybernetic, unthinking servitors that attend the Chapter. Unknown to most, the Grey Knights also maintain large bodies of mortal psykers, scribes, scholars of the occult and many more whose hushed whispers, burdened steps or distant chants are heard among candlelit corridors. Hardened against any partial truths they witness, and often mind-scrubbed for safety, these servants help to maintain the Citadel of Titan's sanctity against daemonic intrusion, amongst many other duties.

BROTHERHOODS

The bulk of the Grey Knights' battle-brothers are organised into eight grand brotherhoods. Each brotherhood comprises a notional one hundred Grey Knights under the overall authority of its Grand Master and the active leadership of its Brother-Captain. His command is usually supported by the brotherhood's Champion, its Ancient and occasionally other officers. The warriors of each brotherhood are marshalled into squads of ten, each led by an experienced veteran granted the title of Justicar. Each squad is tactically flexible, capable of deploying in missions as half-strength combat squads. Squads remain effective and battle-worthy even when so divided, allowing the brotherhood's commanders to tackle multiple threats as efficiently as possible.

Every Grey Knight is trained in the use of the Chapter's varied and esoteric weapons and wargear, and in each mission squads deploy with different tactical loadouts and entrusted with varying strategic objectives. The breakdown of squad type in a given situation is determined by the brotherhood's Grand Master and Brother-Captain. It has long been proven, however, that a balance of Terminator and Strike Squads, supported by Interceptors and Purgation Squads, is by far the most effective combination.

CHAPTER COMMAND

The Grey Knights are governed and directed by the Chapter Council, made up of the Chapter Lord, also known as the Supreme Grand Master, and the eight Grand Masters of the brotherhoods. The council meet in person rarely, for its members often fight far from Titan. Each member has an equal voice, though the Chapter Lord has the responsibility to pass final judgement.

Each Grand Master also holds sway over one of the Chapter's constituent bodies, such as its Armoury or Librarius. Each institution is nominally held to form part of his brotherhood, though he despatches elements of these organisations to undertake extended duties with others. This authority, only partly ceremonial, is tied to the command of a particular brotherhood, and over time the association has informed their fighting style and tactics.

CHAPTER EXEMPLARS

The Grey Knights maintain two further fighting bodies and other honoured positions. Answerable directly to the Chapter Council, they accompany forces at the request of the Grand Masters. The Order of Purifiers rarely numbers more than fifty, and is a cloistered brotherhood with its own traditions whose spiritually pure warriors are led by Knights of the Flame. The Paladins are the Chapter's martial elite, a company of some hundred or so of the most skilled warriors, from whose ranks is selected the Grey Knight's most honoured Ancient. Chaplains lead the Chapter in prayer during gatherings in the Hall of Champions, and it is there also that the wisdom and knowledge of Venerable Dreadnoughts is often sought.

BROTHERS IN COMMUNION

The Grey Knights maintain many of the same specialist roles as other Space Marines. Librarians exercise greater and more diverse psychic powers than most Grey Knights, and help to hone the powers of their battle-brothers. Techmarines have trained with the Tech-Priests of Mars, whose techno-religious strictures the Techmarines balance with the Grey Knights' needs. They maintain the Chapter's vehicles and help craft the psychically imbued wargear its warriors wield. Apothecaries, meanwhile, oversee the creation of new Grey Knights with arcane genetic implantation, as well as healing the most terrible of warp-infected injuries and contagions with medicus tools and chirurgical rituals.

These warriors are assigned to fight alongside one of the Grey Knights' brotherhoods – often for their entire lives – and in certain cases may even be granted command to lead strikes themselves. They are as embedded in their brotherhood's traditional rites and rituals as all its warriors, and lend their considerable skills to its successful prosecution of the daemon. Though assigned to a particular brotherhood, these specialist officers may have completed their training under the auspices of another Grand Master. The Chapter's Armoury, for example, traditionally falls under the rule of the 1st Brotherhood's Grand Master, and he has ultimate responsibility for the Techmarines' Chapter duties.

My lord, subsequent to my most recent holo-transmission from Grand Master Leorac, the data-aureole around this message reveals the extent of our corroborated knowledge regarding the Grey Knights' strategic deployments following the Chapter's feats on Sortiarius.
- [data protocols missing], Inquisitorial Representative to the 666th Chapter, Adeptus Astartes

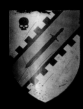

Chapter Council

Chapter Lord Kaldor Draigo,
Supreme Grand Master

Hall of Champions

High Paladin Koiar Tempus, *Paragon Prime*

Grand Masters of the Eight Brotherhoods

Chambers of Purity

Castellan Garran Crowe, *Champion of the Order of Purifiers*

1st Brotherhood

'The Swordbearers'

Grand Master Vardan Kai,
Steward of the Armoury

Brother-Captain Cadrig Pelenas

The Swordbearers were last reported across six war zones in Segmentum Tempestus, hunting dark magi and their warp forges in sectors adjacent to the Siren's Storm. These infernal factorums churn out daemon engines and far worse, but the brotherhood's armoured strikes have already exorcised three of these sites.

2nd Brotherhood

'The Blades of Victory'

Grand Master Vorth Mordrak,
Admiral of the Fleet

Brother-Captain Arno Trevan

Grand Master Mordrak leads the Blades of Victory through the systems of the Daeva Consortium, a trading empire in the Imperium Nihilus. Mordrak's swift ships and preternatural assaults have shut down many networks spreading the Gellerpox contagion, but more remain, and a gestalt sentience stirs.

3rd Brotherhood

'The Wardmakers'

Grand Master Aldrik Voldus,
Warden of the Librarius

Brother-Captain Arvann Stern

Though it cost the brotherhood dearly, Brother-Captain Stern was hailed for his actions on the Planet of the Sorcerers that halted a fell ritual of Magnus the Red. Yet the Wardmakers do not rest; they continue to incinerate daemonic incursions that flare up as the taint of Magnus' world seeps outwards.

4th Brotherhood

'The Prescient Brethren'

Grand Master Drystann Cromm,
Keeper of the Augurium

Brother-Captain Ionan Grud

Following the prophecies of the Prognosticars, elements of the Prescient Brethren lead a series of pre-emptive purges against Aeldari conclaves thought to have links to the so-called 'Ynnari cults', in which the brotherhood detects the fateful patterning of convergent daemonic invocation.

5th Brotherhood

'The Preservers'

Grand Master Rothwyr Morvans,
Protector of the Sanctum Sanctorum

Brother-Captain Tauros Hendron

Half of the 5th Brotherhood are despatched to purify the taint of Tra'mawt'ha the Voidmaw, a warp entity festering with its fell kin in the drifting space hulk, *Vector of Ruin*. The remainder, under Grand Master Morvans, are following a desperate series of visions as they race to reach the Nachmund Gauntlet in time.

6th Brotherhood

'The Rapiers'

Grand Master Caddon Varn,
High Seneschal of the Fortress

Brother-Captain Kerda Tannasek

The Rapiers' peerless reputation for precision is relied upon to cleanse the maze-like fortifications of Baranti. Unbeknown to the traitorous regiments stationed there or their xenos T'au paymasters, Baranti's ancient earthworks hold back the warp in this region; severe damage would damn the entire system.

7th Brotherhood

'The Exactors'

Grand Master Covan Leorac,
Representative to the Inquisition

Brother-Captain Darig Tegvar

Responding to an encrypted missive from the Ordo Malleus, the 7th Brotherhood track down the Radical Inquisitor Rea Yollaron. The dangerous genius has surrounded himself with a small empire of requisitioned troops, Inquisitorial operatives and xenos agents. Yet it is his daemonhosts that will damn him.

8th Brotherhood

'The Silver Blades'

Grand Master Aidan Perdron,
Knight Commander of the Recruits

Brother-Captain Mithrac Tor

Alerted by Gatherers seeing more numerous instances of psychic potential, the Silver Blades uncover a plot by an unknown Greater Daemon to seed the Red Fall worlds with its cults. Several remain to be expunged, but the 8th have discovered another layer of lies as the dead cultists bear the mark of the Hydra.

THE BROTHERHOODS

The brotherhoods of the Grey Knights are at the forefront of the endless war to destroy the daemon wherever it rears its unholy visage. The Chapter does not maintain reserve or specialised companies. The grim and exacerbating duty before them means that every brotherhood requires the integral means to scour the taint of warp spawn from any battlefield.

At the head of every brotherhood is the Grand Master, each a spiritual successor to the eight founders of the Chapter. The Grand Master is responsible for mapping out the never-ending war against the immortal denizens of the warp by whatever means he sees fit. He also maintains his brotherhood's many alliances, whether among the Chapter's other bodies, with Imperial organisations thought to treat with the Grey Knights or others with whom the Chapter has especially covert dealings.

By consulting with the Chapter's Prognosticars and heeding their wisdom, the Grand Master determines where his warriors are most needed. His are decisions that save or condemn billions. Though hundreds, if not thousands of foes may fall before a single one of his hundred or so Grey Knights, the Grand Master's brotherhood cannot be everywhere and not all worlds can be saved. Rather than waste time and his warriors' lives, sometimes the Grand Master must ruthlessly excise falling worlds via the cyclonic warheads of an Exterminatus decree. The Grand Master is not solely a strategist, but also a paragon of martial might; his presence on the battlefield is an indicator of the severity of the foe being faced. He leads the fight in the most perilous battles, while in the deployment and command of his brotherhood he is supported by his experienced Brother-Captain.

The Brother-Captain has operational authority of the brotherhood. It is he who determines how the Grand Master's wider strategy is enacted. The Brother-Captain's place on the battlefield is at the very heart of the fighting, where he stands shoulder to shoulder with his brotherhood, as blazing psychic fire bursts from his armoured fingertips. The Brother-Captain has honed his empyric powers so that he can maintain psychic contact with each of his warriors even in the thickest fighting, adapting his tactics and battle lines with precision and subtlety. This allows him to respond to emergent threats far more swiftly than many Imperial commanders.

Senior warriors of the Brother-Captain's command often fight alongside him. The brotherhood's Champion is an exemplar of the divine martial prowess to which all Grey Knights aspire. In suits of artificer-wrought armour and wielding the signature sword that echoes the Chapter's icon, the Brotherhood Champion defends his Captain with peerless skill and stands ready to die in his commander's stead. To the Brotherhood Ancient, meanwhile, is entrusted one of the brotherhood's sacred standards, taken down from the Hall of Champions on Titan and reverently carried into battle. In its shadow, his brothers are roused to even greater feats of heroism, and the Ancient invokes the names and deeds recorded on the banner in the darkest moments of conflict.

RITES AND RITUALS

The Grey Knights often fight the most hellish of battles over maddening landscapes. As warpfire blazes and the screams and whispers of daemons fill the air, the Grey Knights strengthen their psychic communion. By the invocation of mystic rites and the intoning of ritualised chants in the heat of battle, the warriors steel their souls and sharpen their blades. The Justicars who lead each squad hone their warriors' empyric talents and provide a focus for their powers. Every battle-brother learns not only to fight with all kinds of specialised weapons, armour and wargear, but also the rites associated with each pattern of tactical operation his squad could be expected to fight in.

In other Chapters, Terminator armour is a rare and precious resource, restricted to their elite. It is a measure of the Grey Knights' vital duty that they maintain enough suits to equip their entire Chapter should they wish. Secure in suits of bonded ceramite and hardened exoskeleton, Terminator Squads have been known to fight for weeks on end against daemonic hordes. They scythe down swathes of lighter enemies with tempests of explosive ammunition before cleaving apart far larger creatures with Nemesis force weapons attuned to the wielder's unique powers. So armoured, Grey Knights storm fleshy citadels, battle inside raging firestorms and hunt their foe in the labyrinths of space hulks.

More lightly armoured, Strike Squads wear suits of artificer-wrought power armour engraved with sigils of sanctity. They are often tasked before battle with the reconnaissance of sites that may have been hidden even from the Prognosticars or sorcerous lairs too cramped to admit the bulk of their Terminator brothers. The 6th Brotherhood frequently rely on Strike Squads' surgical attacks to divert and disrupt enemy assaults, before using their psychic augmentation to attack as part of the killing strike. The more heavily armed Purgation Squads wield multiple heavy weapons virtually unknown to the wider Imperium. These squads employ their powers to pierce the warp, perceiving threats through layers of deception. Some Purgators gaze into their foes' futures, seeing so clearly where they will be that they make virtually impossible shots. Grey Knights are often heavily outnumbered, but supported by Purgators, this isn't the case for long.

Many Grey Knight attacks are characterised by the flare of teleportation strikes, their warriors specially fortified against the immaterium's touch. Interceptor Squads brave repeated warp transitions to rapidly redeploy, and intone carefully measured rites that flow between the squad's minds; these allow them to achieve incredible harmonies of empyric coordination their luckless and shocked enemies will never know.

CHAMBER OF TRIALS

It is from the Chamber of Trials that the Company of Gatherers set out across the galaxy in search of recruits. The Gatherers are Grey Knights whose great age or crippling injuries no longer permit them to undertake the primary work of the Chapter, but whose keen minds can winnow out the most suitable aspirants. From among the throngs of prospective candidates their recruitment harvests trawl, the Gatherers select those whose potential is strongest. There are few limits to the harvesters' remit; in their long hunts, they scour many likely sources of recruits: barbaric worlds with no ken of the Imperium; the Black Ships that collect tithes of psykers; civilised worlds of billions where they work via emissaries ignorant of the Grey Knights; even the recruiting worlds of other Space Marine Chapters – commonly without their knowledge.

The Chamber of Trials is where aspirants arrive and their training begins. Even those whose suitable talent and purity are detected by the Gatherers will be weeded out if their fortitude is found wanting. The knowledge and gene-seed a Grey Knight receives – known as the Emperor's Gift – is too valuable to risk wasting, and barely one in a thousand survives the first rite of passage: the pilgrimage through the haunted plains of Xanadu Regio. Most who do are slain in the second rite, during which they must trek through the pitch-black, glyphite-stalked caverns beneath Ganesa Macula. Many more trials await, and a fraction of novitiates make it through the physical and mental challenges to be deemed worthy of receiving the Emperor's Gift and beginning the transformation to Grey Knight.

Chapter Apothecaries, aided by psy-bonded serfs and medicae servitors, implant the Chapter's novitiates with the Grey Knights' unique organs in the lowest levels of the Chamber of Trials. Once these agonising procedures are complete, the novitiate is ordained as a neophyte and his true training begins. Unlike those of most Chapters, Grey Knight neophytes do not serve in battle, for they must endure many years of martial and mental preparation before they can face the most dangerous foe of Titan's sons. A neophyte's skills are sharpened by the Brotherhood Champions and his psychic powers honed by the Librarians. He must also perform the Rituals of Detestation that harden his heart against the lies and temptations of daemons. Should he pass these final challenges, the neophyte will be raised to the rank of Knight and take his place in the fight against Chaos.

Incorruptibility is a terrifying absolute. I who have fought the horrors of the warp, I who have seen others of my Ordo fall from grace, I shudder with thanks at these fearless paragons.

THE WARDMAKERS

THE 3RD BROTHERHOOD

The 3rd Brotherhood of the Grey Knights have won triumphant victories in some of the most dire episodes ever withheld from Imperial records. The breadth of forbidden knowledge they maintain has aided the banishment of the deadliest daemons, and the brotherhood's ancient association with the Chapter's Librarians sees the Wardmakers boast more erudition than any other.

The Wardmakers undertake scholarly research during the brief moments between fighting and martial training. The brotherhood delve into tomes of lore amassed fraction by fraction over the millennia. They learn to craft psychic abjurations with their minds that reject the enslaving psychic yokes of daemons. Many master the rites by which they project their own purifying auras. Some have even become experts in isolating heretics from daemonic overlords that seek to corrupt them further with tainted whispers, severing the foul connections between them. Successive Grand Masters have taught that daemons can be defeated with broad and diverse knowledge, for those creatures ever rely on deceit, misdirection and falsehoods.

A battle-brother of the Wardmakers does not neglect his martial skill in any way, however, honing them under the stern gaze of the brotherhood's learned champion. Only when he can intone the six hundred and sixty-six verses of the Cabalos Luminar without pause or error,

as the champion and a dozen Luna-class combat servitors attack the battle-brother en masse, is he satisfied.

As every Grand Master has an equal voice within the Chapter Council, so every brotherhood is equal; though their associations and methods may differ, none is held above another. It is without doubt, however, that the Wardmakers have been pivotal in defeating the forces of Chaos in countless terrible events. Had but one of these hidden battles been lost, Mankind's future may have been far darker.

When a mysterious infection descended on the Decimalus System, it was the wise counsel of the 3rd's Grand Master at the time, Valdar Aurikon, that revealed a Tzeentchian daemon's machinations at its heart. With careful assessment of Prognosticar readings, Emperor's Tarot and ancient prophecies, he uncovered the disease's implications and its threads of fate. All of this showed it for the titanic threat it truly was: a plague of madness that would have spread without end.

On Kalva V, the Wardmakers faced daemons of all four Chaos Gods in an incursion that spilled towards the Segmentum Fortress at Cypra Mundi. The brotherhood faced legions of daemon engines, too, and possessed husks that were all that was left of the former populace. The 3rd Brotherhood drew deep from their vast knowledge, crafting sorceries that were tailored to every foul iteration of daemon crawling before them, for no one sanctified blast could have cut through all the differing forms.

It was under the nascent command of Grand Master Voldus that the 3rd Brotherhood stood side by side with the Ultramarines on Macragge. Their empyric powers threw back Chaos sorcery during the Siege of Hera and ensured the successful resurrection of the Primarch, Roboute Guilliman.

ALDRIK VOLDUS

Grand Master Voldus wields more psychic might than any Grey Knight seen in centuries. Where he strides into

battle, the air grows heavy with empyric charges and he unleashes his powers in waves of purifying flame that scour the foe before him. His relic daemon hammer, the Malleus Argyrum, was crafted over the course of a century by the blind smith Hulliver. Thrumming as Voldus feeds psychic power into its arcane core, the Grand Master wields it as if it weighs nothing at all, and his attacks strike with the force of a thunderbolt.

His elevation to the vaunted position of Grand Master of the 3rd Brotherhood came during the onset of the Great Rift's apocalyptic emergence. Though his ennoblement came from the lips of Lord Kaldor Draigo himself in the wake of their combined banishment of a Tzeentchian daemonic lord, it is one that sits heavily with Voldus. He sees himself as a humble warrior who sought no greater advancement than a position from which to slay the hated daemon. Yet he swore Lord Draigo an oath to live up to the honour, and on Macragge, on Gathalamor Prime, on Luna and Holy Terra itself among many others, Aldrik Voldus has proven – at least to others – his supreme ability, strength and will.

As well as commanding a brotherhood of the most elite Space Marines, Voldus is Warden of the Librarius. In this capacity, he has authority over the Chapter's Librarians and the dangerous archives of knowledge that they guard.

ARVANN STERN

Amongst the Grey Knights' ranks, Brother-Captain Stern stands as one of the longest-serving and most decorated. On Atraxes, Stern led the counter-attack that culled the Cult of the Red Talon. He alone cornered M'kachen, the Lord of Change that enslaved them, and banished the screaming daemon back to the warp in a psychic feat thought beyond the capacity of a lone Brother-Captain.

So began a vendetta of centuries in which M'kachen has seemed to interfere in the redoubtable Brother-Captain's fate; for each of Stern's heroic feats some dire misfortune befalls his allies. Since Atraxes, the daemon has haunted his steps. Each time they have fought,

M'kachen has managed to flee, killing many of Stern's battle-brothers before he does so. Yet with each confrontation, Stern learns more of his daemonic nemesis as, no doubt, the daemon believes it learns more of him in turn. Stern has refused any advancement until the threat of M'kachen can be ended forever. When the daemon overreaches itself, so Stern has sworn, it will be his blade that avenges his fallen brothers.

LIBRARIANS

Every Grey Knight is a psyker, a bearer of a mutation that sets him as much apart from other Space Marines as his genetically enhanced body sets him apart from Humanity. But few of the Chapter's battle-brothers exercise this power with free rein – even for a Grey Knight this would offer a way into the material realm for insatiable daemons. It is the Librarians who train their brothers to focus their psychic gifts in concert with others of their squad.

The Chapter's Librarians are experts in the use of their powers. They are capable of invoking all manner of diverse incantations. These they build up over

centuries of arcane study and mental duels with creatures from the warp. Librarians are assigned to fight alongside one of the brotherhoods, supporting their brother Grey Knights on the battlefield and offering counsel on matters of obscure lore. As part of controlling their own powers, Librarians are skilled in resisting the insidious influence of the warp. They wear complex cowls – amalgams of crystal and neural wiring – that empower them in tearing apart the sorceries of others.

Librarians maintain ancient titles or ranks, the origins of which are uncertain. As he rises through this hierarchy, from Lexicanium to Codicier and thence Epistolary, the Librarian is judged stronger in mind. He becomes more capable of wielding dangerous power and is granted access to some of the darkest mysteries held by the Chapter.

LIBRARIUM DAEMONICA

Located deep in the Sanctum Sanctorum lies the Librarium Daemonica. It is one of the most heavily shielded and guarded locations in the Imperium, for here lies the Grey Knights' corpus of knowledge on daemonkind. Some of the lore predates the Imperium or has been obtained from long-dead xenos races, and some is reputed to have been dictated by Malcador or even the Emperor himself.

The threat of such knowledge falling into the wrong hands is not underestimated. The Librarium Daemonica lies behind three adamantine barriers, each many yards thick, protected by enchantments, anointed with consecrated oils and etched with silver seals of warding. Elder Librarians guard each of the three massive portals, the gateways sealed with layers of arcane ciphers, spatial displacers and magical vortices. Any seeking entrance who does not utter the secret words of passage at the ritualised moment will be destroyed by the guardian Librarians without pause. Among the dread knowledge contained within are the True Names of many of the foulest daemons, and the known instances of their manifestations. One, the daemon known as M'kachen, is unpleasantly familiar to the 3rd's Brother-Captain, for its fate and his are inextricably linked.

1st Brotherhood

'The Swordbearers'

The Grand Master of the 1st holds the title of Steward of the Armoury, with nominal guardianship of the Chapter's Techmarines who maintain and administer the Chapter's engines of war. The 1st Brotherhood regularly undertake hammerblow strikes with great numbers of the Chapter's reserves of Land Raiders, Stormhawk Interceptors, and Stormtalon and Stormraven Gunships. As such, the Swordbearers are often called upon when the Grey Knights require armoured or aerial support, and in their ranks are many of the finest pilots of the Chapter. Many of the Chapter's Techmarines fight alongside the 1st Brotherhood after completing their training, fulfilling their battlefield duties under the same Grand Master who oversees their wider commitments to the Chapter's sacred fighting vehicles. The battle-brothers of the Swordbearers are drilled to fight in perfect unison with these hallowed war machines, shattering the ranks of the enemy to allow barrages of stormstrike missiles and godhammer lascannon fire to blast apart towering Greater Daemons as they manifest from the warp onto the battlefield.

2nd Brotherhood

'The Blades of Victory'

The Blades of Victory have a well-deserved reputation for rapid deployment and swift strikes, even by the standards of the Grey Knights. The brotherhood makes use of large numbers of Interceptor and Strike Squads, using mass teleportation tactics to outmanoeuvre their enemies. The 2nd is often in the vanguard of combined brotherhood assaults, bursting onto the battlefield to form a beachhead and seeding the way for heavier troops to follow. As Admiral of the Fleet, the Grand Master of the 2nd excels at the art of military manoeuvres and formation, ensuring the Grey Knights' rapid deployment to a war zone. With the predictions of the Prognosticars providing vital tactical information, Grey Knight strike cruisers and battle barges –deploying elements of the 2nd Brotherhood – are often able to deliver forces to the battlefield before the foe has even made its arrival. The current Grand Master, Vorth Mordrak, is said to be circled by the psychic echoes of the fallen, given deathly form by his innate powers. Though he has sworn to find the reason for their ghostly presence, the greater mission of the Chapter always comes first.

3rd Brotherhood

'The Wardmakers'

The Wardmakers have always held a place of honour within the Chapter. It was, according to legend, Janus' own brotherhood, and throughout the long history of the Grey Knights it has fostered many of the Chapter's greatest heroes. Kaldor Draigo was Brother-Captain and then Grand Master of the 3rd. The Wardmakers' Grand Master is concurrently the Warden of the Librarius, a position renowned for being dangerous and perhaps even cursed. Voldus' predecessor, Doriam Narathem, was slain mere missions into his tenure by M'kachen, the same Lord of Change that seeks to ensnare Arvann Stern, the Wardmakers' Brother-Captain. The Grand Master has authority over the Chapter's Librarians, and thus his responsibility and influence are felt in every brotherhood. Many of these Librarians fight alongside the 3rd Brotherhood in battle and, through their guidance, the Wardmakers employ great psychic flexibility, made possible by being steeped in many of the subtlest and least known Chapter rituals. The brotherhood are capable of adapting their mental attack patterns as swiftly as their warriors switch tactical strategies.

4th Brotherhood

'The Prescient Brethren'

The Keeper of the Augurium commands the 4th Brotherhood, and within its ranks are many of the Chapter's most potent psykers – warriors with an instinctual understanding of the warp that goes beyond even that of their peers. It is from the Prescient Brethren that new Prognosticars are often chosen, yet only if they have shown particular aptitude and are considered too valuable an asset to risk on the battlefield. Members of the Prescient Brethren often have the ability to sense danger before it materialises, and they use this to stalk their enemy relentlessly and to devise highly effective ambushes in which to snare their foe. Such abilities are of the utmost value when combating daemons – creatures whose timeless and unnatural existences allow many to manipulate the strands of fate – as well as races such as the meddlesome Aeldari. The ability to anticipate their enemies' manoeuvres also enhances their martial abilities, and some of the greatest duellists in the Chapter's history have come from the Prescient Brethren. Few are the swordsmen whose skill can outmatch empyric foreknowledge.

5ᵗʰ Brotherhood
'The Preservers'

The responsibility of the Chapter's greatest legacy, its gene-seed, lies with the Grand Master of the 5th, for it is under his auspices that Apothecaries are trained in their vital duties. Not only that but, as Protector of the Sanctum Sanctorum, his is the responsibility for the preservation of numerous strands of knowledge, including the unique technological and historical lore housed there. The living embodiments of much of this data are the Grey Knights' Dreadnoughts, in which form warriors too injured to be healed continue to serve. To be Grand Master of the 5th, in many ways the warden of these ancients, requires great humility, for many Dreadnoughts house battle-brothers with experience dating back millennia. By tradition, fallen warriors newly entombed inside Dreadnought sarcophagi often fight alongside the 5th while they learn through combat how to wield the raw power of their machine spirit. Where the Preservers battle, their strategies are often centred on these honoured ancients. The ground shakes beneath pounding iron feet as the fury of these deathless war machines is brutally released upon those before them.

6ᵗʰ Brotherhood
'The Rapiers'

The Grey Knights do not tolerate wasted effort or manpower, and in the history-making deliberations of the Chapter Council it is often the High Seneschal of the Fortress who is tasked with crafting the most elite and deadly strike forces. Those who serve as High Seneschal are stringent taskmasters, their dedication to excellence and efficiency reflected in the warriors of their brotherhood. The Rapiers are exemplars in the creation of strategically deployed, purpose-built strike forces, able to inflict as much damage as far larger armies. Rather than using destructive orbital bombardments and mass teleportation, the Rapiers rely on surgical strikes, trusting the training and expertise of small squads of specialists to get the job done. Where bulk of numbers is necessary, the Grand Master or his Brother-Captain deploys mindless servitors to bog down the enemy, allowing his Grey Knights to focus on high-risk targets. Records kept solely within the Citadel of Titan even reveal the expert yet ruthless factoring of other unsuspecting Imperial forces into some of the Rapiers' most finely executed strikes. If such loss is lauded as noble sacrifice, so be it.

7ᵗʰ Brotherhood
'The Exactors'

The Inquisition and the Grey Knights were founded, according to some sources, around the same time. Though created to act independently of one another, many goals of the two orders broadly align. The Exactors have a long history of acting upon information supplied by the Ordo Malleus, occasionally alongside them; as a result, respected Inquisitors are often able to call upon them for aid. It is through the Grand Master, as Representative to the Inquisition, that contact usually flows. In return, the Exactors expect the Inquisition to provide watchful eyes throughout the Imperium, and to supply them with auxiliary forces whenever and wherever they request them. The 7th Brotherhood sometimes fights alongside Imperial troops requisitioned by the Inquisition, utilising platoons of Astra Militarum soldiers to hold key battlefield positions or Inquisitorial Acolytes to quell daemonic uprisings. Those brave troops who survive their missions with the Exactors, and somehow avoid the Inquisitorial purges that follow, continue to serve the Chapter as mind-scoured servitors, as long as their biological components retain their integrity.

8ᵗʰ Brotherhood
'The Silver Blades'

When a newly forged battle-brother joins the ranks of the Grey Knights, he will typically be sequestered to the 8th Brotherhood. He may then find a place within one of the other brotherhoods, depending on his natural talents and the favour of the Grand Masters, or he may choose to remain with the Silver Blades. Those who remain dedicate themselves to continual training, running the trials of initiation again and again in the pursuit of martial perfection. Led by the Knight Commander of the Recruits, the warriors of the 8th fight in fluid configurations, changing tactics swiftly during combat and between engagements. Any available weapon is put to use, and no strategy or manoeuvre is preferred over any other. A Silver Blade aims to be proficient in the use of every armament, and to know the strength in every strike force and the weakness in every enemy. It is to the Grand Master of the 8th that the Company of Gatherers and their Master also report, and the Silver Blades ever look out for survivors who appear unusually determined and free of taint. Such individuals regularly pique the interest of the Inquisition as well, and debates on the length of their futures run hot.

The Plaguebearer's foul breath enveloped Justicar Thorem as it leaned in close to him. Dozens more inexorably pressed forward in a suffocating mass, hacking with sweeping blows against Thorem's battle-brothers who fought at his side, pushing upstream against a flow of knee-high filth along the Kromtoid Ravine. The daemon's clawed free hand grasped Thorem's pauldron with unnatural strength, the rotten warp-stuff of its fingers blistering and fizzing where it touched the blessed battle-plate.

The daemon's heavy blade scraped along Thorem's Nemesis force sword. Blisters rose and burst on the rusted plaguesword's surface in flakes of pus-brown metal that blew away from the Grey Knight in the psychic radiance of his Aegis. His force sword gripped in two gauntleted hands, Thorem pitted his augmented strength against the Plaguebearer's rotten simulacra of muscle, tendons and bones. He began the recitation of the Canticle of Absolution, in psychic communion with his squad.

Praise the Emperor for his sacrifice, as he endures so shall we.

The noise of battle and the droning of flies surrounding the daemons rang from the walls of the Kromtoid Ravine, where they fought the Grey Knights beneath Remiga Hive. At the ravine's head lay the squad's objective: the Mallacopia, the source of the daemonic effluvia pouring into this world. The Prognosticars had foreseen that the artefact would forge a connection with the warp, opening a rift out of which the immaterium's contamination would spew, until this world was nothing but an orb of oily pus.

Echoes of detonations from the far-distant surface reached Thorem's helm, catching up with the aerial vid-feed displayed on his inner visor. Half a mile above him, on the surface, the planet's defence forces fought a futile containment action against daemons pouring from the fallen Remiga Hive. While monitoring the surface battle, orbital auguries from Thorem's shrouded ship directed his squad to the hydro basilica where Remiga's macroduct network suckled at glacial runoff. There, the Prognosticars' vision suggested, lay the source of the world's infection.

We shall seek out the Tainted, we shall pursue the Vilest Evil.

If the Prognosticars' visions were accurate, Thorem saw he had little time before the next violent cycle of the Mallacopia's exudation. He girded his soul, his psychic aura coalescing at his core, strengthened by those around him. Shimmering, azure circlets with patterns of swirling characters span around his arms. Thorem formed the psychic lattices of the Thirty-third Rite of Sequestration,

speaking the mantra of its invocation while feeding more power into his Nemesis blade.

At the speed of rigorously disciplined thought, Thorem had taken mere fractions of a second to review his tactical displays, commune with his squad and invoke the rite. The Justicar could see the daemon's discomfort and, he hoped, even fear. Beneath a protruding horn, its enlarged, rheumy eye wavered as if momentarily insubstantial. Its flesh darkened, disintegrating in fragments the longer it forced itself into close proximity with his sanctified aura.

Thorem pushed his mental construct forwards. The Plaguebearer's fleshy face shrivelled, its swollen eye boiled. With a savage twist and rapid reverse stroke, Thorem broke the plaguesword in two and drove his own blade up through the Plaguebearer's bloated gut and into its head. He released the built-up power in the sword's psycho-crystalline matrices, channelling spears of purifying energy into the daemon's form. The Plaguebearer burned. Its flesh turned to ash, collapsing into a fading point through the potent effects of the rite.

More of the Plaguebearers fell to Thorem's Strike Squad. The Justicar saw that their hold on realspace was waning, lumps of their flesh crumbling into the knee-high slurry that flowed from behind them. Their emaciated limbs belied their power, but their filthy blades could not penetrate the Grey Knights' warded ceramite, instead only scoring the power armour in desperate strikes.

Thorem swept back into the wavering daemons, pouring his psychic might into his squad's collective aura. The clouds of flies shrank as they burst into miniature balls of blue fire in the Grey Knights' purifying aurora. Even as their resilient flesh was rent apart, the Plaguebearers were driven by a malign will to endure and survive.

We shall be Pure amongst Impurity, we shall be Innocence amongst Guilt.

A Grey Knight wielding a fire-wreathed warding stave bludgeoned the final cyclopean visage. The daemon dissolved into a sickly mist. This had been only the latest in a series of attacks the Grey Knights had lanced through as they made for the Mallacopia. With them destroyed, Thorem's auto senses detected the growl of giant machinery not far from their position, confirming the data-screed from orbit. He signalled to the rest of the squad.

'Quickly, brothers. The hydro basilica is ahead,' he voxed.

Pumping Station Deltic IV sprawled across the width of the Kromtoid Ravine. Before the rusted facade of the hydro basilica, a string of seven conduit junctions the size of fortress redoubts fed massive pipe networks into the crevasse floor. Behind Deltic IV, these macroducts were embedded into the Ravine's wall, up which they ran to water Remiga Hive. The filth was several feet deep here, and a shallow mound of corpses rose from it.

Hundreds of the dead were jammed together, in various states of decay. Thorem saw that many retained remnants of filthy robes and the trappings of Chaos worship. He recognised the sigils raised in weals upon their faces as tributes for a rite of summoning. Whatever evil dwelled here, the Justicar realised, these heretics had called it.

Upon the mound's centre was the Mallacopia. It appeared as three horns of some giant beast, melded together. From their hollow, gaping mouths, filth poured in a torrent.

'You are not invited to our feast. Yet since you offer yourselves so freely, you may be part of it instead,' roared a chorus of voices.

From the other side of the mound, a corpulent figure, taller and broader than Thorem, strode to the side of the Mallacopia. Pustules and buboes riddled its mass of festering flesh and rigid, bony growths sprouted from its bent spine. Three heads jostled upon his hunched shoulders, each split by a fang-filled mouth. Only the central head bore eyes: a cluster like three weeping sores.

There is no Chaos-spawned horror that can resist our indomitable anger.

Thorem's squad advanced on the corpse pile. This was the source of the infection, the Justicar saw, the place from which the Mallacopia's noisome vomit must have pushed up the macroducts into Remiga Hive, drowning millions. Thorem's warp sight now perceived the pulsing, feverish glare of the daemon's unique psychic aura. To one versed in the mysteries of the Index Urshad in the Librarium Daemonica, it was a reliable identification.

I know you now, he thought. *Your foul essence betrays you.*

The squad unleashed a hail of bolts without slowing their pace as the daemon moved to shield the Mallacopia. It snatched at the air with a clawed hand before they hit. A dozen bolts swerved, flung aside by warp magic, but many hit home. They blew chunks from its flesh, but the ruptured craters pulsed as new growths pushed through from within.

The warp-spawn reached behind it, pulling one of the growths from its back and pointing the long shard at the Grey Knights like a gnarled wand. Babbles of meaningless numerology came from each mouth and it gestured to the flowing lake of dark ooze around them. Thorem felt the surge of sorcery and he sent a pulse of thought outwards.

Brothers, the Circle of the Sixth Abjuration, now.

The squad moved into practiced warding positions as waves and unhealthy froth formed. Suddenly, the liquid stuff of the warp rose up around the Grey Knights.

Before the towering waves of noxious substance could swamp them, Thorem's warriors thrust their psychic rejection of diabolic power outwards. The liquid miasma was held. It churned in suspension above them and coiling shapes thrashed inside, trying to pierce their ward.

No corruption shall blemish our Galaxy, no Immaterial Fiend shall be spared.

Thorem allowed the daemon no time to renew or adapt its thwarted sorcery. While his battle-brothers held back the towering walls of filth, he balanced their power as a nexus at their centre, and began a curse that had been prepared at the mission's very inception.

'I denounce you, abomination, *In Nomine Veritas!*'

The Mallacopia was not all the Prognosticars had foreseen. They had beheld Urg'thorrg'urhraslem the Tribane in the same vision, but nothing was certain. Until he had seen the three-headed Herald, Thorem had not known if the True Name he had prepared had been worth the risk. To learn even a shard of such knowledge was dangerous.

'Ger'sh-vrrewg'shaa'a, thry'goyqe'kraneg–', Thorem began.

The daemon spasmed as realisation of Thorem's purpose dawned upon it. Portions of the Name-shard were intoned psychically, others required the remoulding of his larynx with biomancy, sounds that would flense the sanity of lesser beings. Two of the daemon's heads exploded and the tidal waves of filth collapsed. The daemon fell to its knees, shaking in palsy as Thorem strode up the mound of corpses. The Justicar's Nemesis blade glowed with the righteousness of his imminent deed.

No Spawn of Misrule avoids us, all are banished to the void.

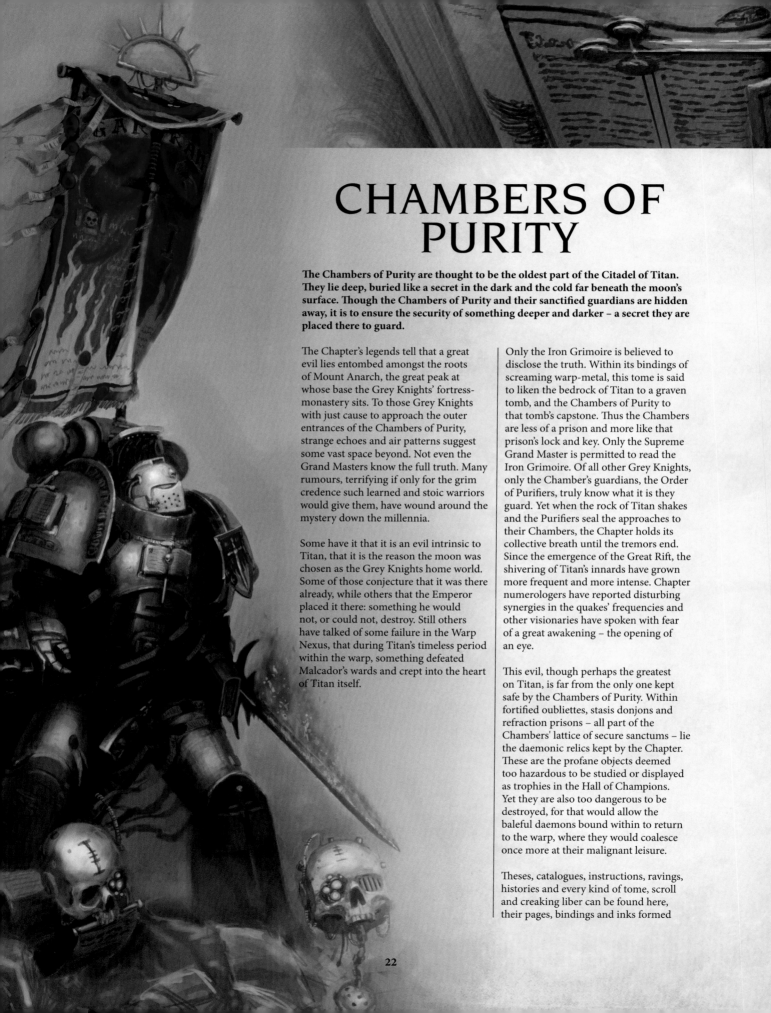

CHAMBERS OF PURITY

The Chambers of Purity are thought to be the oldest part of the Citadel of Titan. They lie deep, buried like a secret in the dark and the cold far beneath the moon's surface. Though the Chambers of Purity and their sanctified guardians are hidden away, it is to ensure the security of something deeper and darker – a secret they are placed there to guard.

The Chapter's legends tell that a great evil lies entombed amongst the roots of Mount Anarch, the great peak at whose base the Grey Knights' fortress-monastery sits. To those Grey Knights with just cause to approach the outer entrances of the Chambers of Purity, strange echoes and air patterns suggest some vast space beyond. Not even the Grand Masters know the full truth. Many rumours, terrifying if only for the grim credence such learned and stoic warriors would give them, have wound around the mystery down the millennia.

Some have it that it is an evil intrinsic to Titan, that it is the reason the moon was chosen as the Grey Knights home world. Some of those conjecture that it was there already, while others that the Emperor placed it there: something he would not, or could not, destroy. Still others have talked of some failure in the Warp Nexus, that during Titan's timeless period within the warp, something defeated Malcador's wards and crept into the heart of Titan itself.

Only the Iron Grimoire is believed to disclose the truth. Within its bindings of screaming warp-metal, this tome is said to liken the bedrock of Titan to a graven tomb, and the Chambers of Purity to that tomb's capstone. Thus the Chambers are less of a prison and more like that prison's lock and key. Only the Supreme Grand Master is permitted to read the Iron Grimoire. Of all other Grey Knights, only the Chamber's guardians, the Order of Purifiers, truly know what it is they guard. Yet when the rock of Titan shakes and the Purifiers seal the approaches to their Chambers, the Chapter holds its collective breath until the tremors end. Since the emergence of the Great Rift, the shivering of Titan's innards have grown more frequent and more intense. Chapter numerologers have reported disturbing synergies in the quakes' frequencies and other visionaries have spoken with fear of a great awakening – the opening of an eye.

This evil, though perhaps the greatest on Titan, is far from the only one kept safe by the Chambers of Purity. Within fortified oubliettes, stasis donjons and refraction prisons – all part of the Chambers' lattice of secure sanctums – lie the daemonic relics kept by the Chapter. These are the profane objects deemed too hazardous to be studied or displayed as trophies in the Hall of Champions. Yet they are also too dangerous to be destroyed, for that would allow the baleful daemons bound within to return to the warp, where they would coalesce once more at their malignant leisure.

Theses, catalogues, instructions, ravings, histories and every kind of tome, scroll and creaking liber can be found here, their pages, bindings and inks formed

of a thousand substances – few of them given willingly. Bones there are too, of fallen 'saints' and enslaving prophet-hawkers, of possessed xenos tyrants such as those of the Whisperer, whose unearthing by a greed-driven Inquisitor brought about the Plague of Madness. Tainted energies in grav-suspension, xenos technologies and mechanical idols from darker ages languish in bonds, their sentiences raging or else repeating unheeded pleas of innocence. Blades, hooks, maces, strangely proportioned firearms and countless other forms of life-taker are sequestered in gilded caskets. These daemon weapons have tasted blood and souls and are some of the Chambers' most dangerous occupants, their will kept dormant by the workings of ancient technology and the powerful radiance of the Chambers' keepers.

ORDER OF PURIFIERS

The Purifiers are an organisation apart from other Grey Knights, distanced from their battle-brothers by their nature and tradition. They guard the Chambers of Purity against mortal and immortal incursion, ensuring nothing and no one breaches their realm to reach the mountains' roots beyond. Only the Grand Masters of the brotherhoods and the Chapter Lord are permitted within their domain unbidden and none at all any further. They have the authority and determination to destroy any who are not permitted. In the rare instances of intruders, none have returned, their fate remaining unknown and unquestioned.

The Purifiers epitomise the Chapter's sanctity of purpose. There is neither training regime nor set process by which a Grey Knight joins their dour and taciturn ranks. Membership of the Order of Purifiers is not granted through skill, valour or a tally of grim deeds, and a Grey Knight may serve with unblemished distinction throughout his functionally immortal lifetime without being granted this singular honour. Rather, Purifiers recruit only from those Grey Knights whose souls are held to be utterly incorruptible – even beyond the usual exacting standards of the Chapter. So painstaking is the selection and so rarely bestowed that there are seldom more than a few score of Purifiers. Whether

it be by some quirk of mystical fate, however, their numbers seldom drop so low as to render their duties unfulfilled. Thus, never has thought been given to relaxing the restrictions of induction, lest the sanctity of the order be compromised.

On rare occasions, the head of the Purifier order will accede to a request from one of the Grand Masters for the aid of a portion of their warriors. Only one of the Council can make such a demand. Understanding the gravity of the Purifiers' duty, even while not knowing its true nature, a Grand Master does so only in the direst of circumstances.

When Purifiers deploy, they often form the Chapter's spearhead in war zones that boil and churn with legions of daemons. The Purifiers' untarnished spirit is not only their defining characteristic – it is also their greatest weapon. Like the light of battle said to halo the Imperium's greatest saints, a nimbus of radiance illuminates these pure warriors. Combined with a Grey Knight's formidable psychic might, this inviolability of heart and mind is transformed into a cleansing, azure fire that burns unworthy adversaries in body and soul. Little resists the power of this glorious conflagration. A daemon's cold malignancy is turned violently against it; a corrupted soldier's fear erupts into a corona of fire; and the malevolence of predatory xenos consumes such aliens. None but the Purifiers walk unharmed through this blaze, armour gleaming as they despatch of their charred foes.

CASTELLAN CROWE

Garran Crowe, the Champion of the Order of Purifiers, is both its head and its guiding spirit. He is – by any measure of the Grey Knights – a flawless soul, so resistant to the wiles of Chaos as to be thought immune to them. It is to the keeping of this paragon that the Chapter entrusts one of its most heinous possessions – the Black Blade of Antwyr.

The Black Blade is a daemon weapon of singular power. The entity bound within it had yoked the minds of previous wielders, making bloody war with its slave and their armies in thrall to its will across entire sectors. Though it would disappear for centuries at a time, fleeing with its slave into the warp, the Grey Knights finally slew its bearer and captured it. The Blade of Antwyr, alas, proved so powerful that no craft of the Grey Knights could destroy it. Its corruptive potential was deemed too great even for the Chambers of Purity to contain permanently; perhaps its insistent whispers might infect others on Titan or beyond.

It was seen that the safest prison was the constant grasp of the Purifiers' Champion. From one of these epitomes of sanctity to the next it has passed, and is now in the iron grip of Castellan Crowe. The blade whispers, cajoles and screams constantly, promising undreamt power and threatening vile abasement in a voice only Crowe can hear. At times, it has even offered up aid to him, as he faced one of its daemonic rivals. Crowe must forever be on his guard. When not beset by the mortals and daemons drawn to its influence, the Castellan must do psychic battle with the Blade itself. He listens not to a word of its lies and never responds to its temptations. Unto death, he is its guardian, not its slave.

HALL OF CHAMPIONS

Among rows of iron-bound basalt columns rising to vaulted arches far above the central Hall of Champions hang the standards and trophies of the Grey Knights. Dark statues stare down, their stern countenances underlit by consecrated candles. Along with subsidiary chancels and Council chambers, the Hall forms the Chapter's martial and spiritual heart.

The huge, central chamber of the Citadel of Titan is known as the Hall of Champions, though in truth this term stretches to encompass a warren of chambers, passages and sanctuaries that lead from the central Hall's tiered levels. Here are held rare feasts when more than a handful of Grey Knights are upon Titan together. These are often in the wake of a hard-fought victory, the battle-brothers within the fortress-monastery recovering and re-arming before the next vision of doom calls them to war once more.

Ranks of statues regard ceremonial proceedings, and oaths are sometimes sworn directly to them. They depict the Grey Knights' ancestors: Chapter heroes granted a form of immortality in which to inspire those who take up the fight after them. The Hall is also a place in which to honour living heroes. Investitures and ordinations take place within circles of abjuration inlaid into the solid floor in silver. Trophies taken from the defeated are displayed on sigil-carved iron hooks and chains. These may be shattered weapons, fragments of psy-scorched armour or stranger items like the thirteen twisted iron masks of the Daemon Magi purged from Cebrum II.

Perhaps most unusual of all is the skull of Iremn'ath, the Daemon Rajah of Nalu. Before the defeated creature's spirit could flee to the warp, the Grey Knights bound it into its flayed skull. Now, its fading sentience rages silently and impotently, forced to witness the celebration of the Grey Knights' every triumph over Chaos. Though the Grey Knights' prime concern is the daemonic menace, they fight countless battles against the alien, mutant and heretic and many trophies in the Hall stand as testament to these victories.

PALADINS

The Hall of Champions is the seat of the Paladins – the Grey Knights' greatest warrior squads – and many of the statues there represent former companions of the Paladins' fraternity. As the Order of Purifiers stand as the Grey Knights' sanctified elite, the Paladins are the Chapter's martial exemplars.

If a Grey Knight wishes to prove himself worthy of a place amongst such a lauded elite, bravery and skill at arms are not enough. He must complete eight quests to establish his character and cause. Each more arduous and deadly than the last, they culminate in the hunting down and banishment of one of the six hundred and sixty-six most powerful daemons known to have manifested. Battle-brothers have died on these quests, refusing to abandon them and incur grave dishonour. It is a measure of the Paladins' status that a Grey Knight seeking admission is willing to risk depriving his Chapter of his skills, that he may serve it to a higher standard.

The Paladins seldom fight as one body. The Supreme Grand Master, or one of the Council in his stead, call upon the Paladins when they require the very best of the Chapter to take the field, and they are usually despatched in small numbers to support individual brotherhoods. Truly selfless, yet with the skill to destroy the foulest beasts, Paladins throw themselves without hesitation into combat with towering daemon lords and murderous hordes of warp spawn.

GLORIA IN MEMORIAM

The sacred standards and banners that hang in the Hall of Champions represent every brotherhood and order of the Grey Knights. They honour the cleansing of worlds and the purging of unhallowed evil. There are few in the Imperium that know of such heroics and fewer still who record them. Each brotherhood maintains many standards in the Hall and here also are displayed the personal banners and relics of fallen heroes. The Paladin Ancient has been chosen from amongst that exemplar brotherhood for his reverence and stoicism. In his unshakeable grasp is carried one of the Chapter's greatest standards, one that depicts the Grey Knights' most glorious victories over daemonkind. His is a duty more personal than that of many Ancients, for he has fought in many of these great victories and is as much a figure of inspiration as the banner he lifts.

It is against the stirring backdrop of these standards that the Chapter's Chaplains lead their Brotherhoods in prayer during the greatest gatherings in the Hall of Champions, as they also do before battle. Chaplains are the spiritual leaders of the Grey Knights. They maintain many of the Chapter's traditions and inculcate neophytes in the strictures they must know before acceptance, as well as mercilessly administering punishments to those they perceive as wavering in their focus. Their fiery sermons, shouted over the din of battle or intoned with grim solemnity in the Hall, remind those among whom they fight of the price of failure, psychically reinforcing the heavy duty laid upon them all by the Emperor.

There may be no others with our sanctity of purpose, who combine our singular aim with our undiminished resolution. We were created for this purpose. We do not fear the abominations of Chaos that lie beyond the veneer of reality. It is they who fear us.

· D E U S ·

KALDOR DRAIGO

At the Grand Masters' high table in the Hall of Champions, the place of honour has sat empty since before the opening of the Cicatrix Maledictum. Chapter Lord Kaldor Draigo, the Supreme Grand Master, passed beyond the sight of the Chapter on the world of Acralem. Two hundred years earlier, Draigo defeated the daemon M'kar the Reborn there, and the creature had sworn its revenge. This time, however, as Draigo cast the self same daemon into a warp rift, the creature's spite was not done with him. Screeching a curse two centuries in the making, M'kar's taloned claws dragged Lord Draigo into the warp with it.

If M'kar had hoped Draigo's soul would become a tortured plaything for the denizens of the warp, he had underestimated the Supreme Grand Master. In a way which is still not understood, Draigo survived. His mind and his spirit, hardened against the essence of Chaos over long years, helped him endure where perhaps no other man could.

The Chapter Lord wandered for a timeless age, defeating and crushing every daemon that dared threaten him, rejecting temptations and madness and hardening his will to survive. Yet realspace was not done with Draigo. On Jostero, a heretical warp ritual caused him to be drawn back. There he fought alongside warriors of his Chapter once more but, at battle's end, he could not save himself from sliding back into the warp. Thus has been his fate ever since: drawn back and forth for unknowable periods, fighting endless daemons in both realms. Yet his Chapter know that he lives, and in many battles his sudden appearance has swung victory for the Grey Knights.

WAR ZONE: MANASK

One of many hundreds such expeditions, the Torchbearer Task Force Conqueror's Forge speared through the immaterium like gold, bronze and iron darts flung from Terra. Yet when it neared Manask, the home world of the Ebon Sentinels Chapter, the fleet's passage was abruptly forbidden by Grey Knights of the 8th and 6th Brotherhoods, who locked the system down.

The Ebon Sentinels were a lauded Chapter of the Adeptus Astartes, the defenders of the Sunnan Strait since their founding millennia ago. Though an unrecorded incident early in their history saw them censured, their one-hundred-and-one-year crusade of penance brought so many worlds back to the Imperial fold that a plaque of honour was consecrated upon the cardinal world of Ophelia VII and the Chapter's good name was restored. Records from prior to the opening of the Great Rift revealed their grievous losses of both warriors and ships in gruelling wars, their recruitment struggling to compensate. They were thus amongst the first Chapters of Segmentum Tempestus to be assigned a Torchbearer task force.

Conqueror's Forge was one of an unrecorded number of the vital Torchbearer task forces. They had already made perilous journeys to deliver Archmagos Cawl's arcane science, tonnes of ordnance, armour and war engines to the Astral Spears and Condemnors Chapters, returning to Terra after each expedition. Despatched next to the Manask System, Conqueror's Forge carried Greyshield reinforcements and Primaris technologies to the Ebon Sentinels Chapter. The fleet's mass bulk-hauler and vast ark mechanicus were shepherded by sleek and dangerous destroyers and light cruisers, equipped to ensure the completion of the mission by smashing any foes in their way, but with orders to ignore distracting pleas for aid.

The task force's Navigators maintained a swift route and its Astropaths directed unanswered hails at Manask. Sisters of Silence spread through the ships eased their passage through the warp with their soulless aura. They were not the only esoteric envoys of Terra's will. The Astrolineator who commanded the ark mechanicus held nominal authority over the task force, but beyond oversight of the Primaris technology, emergency powers were wielded by others aboard. Gilded giants of the Adeptus Custodes, a dour Rogue Trader employed as sub-sector pilot and Inquisitor Lord Kavnar of the Emperor's Holy Ordos all stood ready to issue diktats should the need occur.

Known only to the senior Custodian and Inquisitor, a second flotilla shadowed

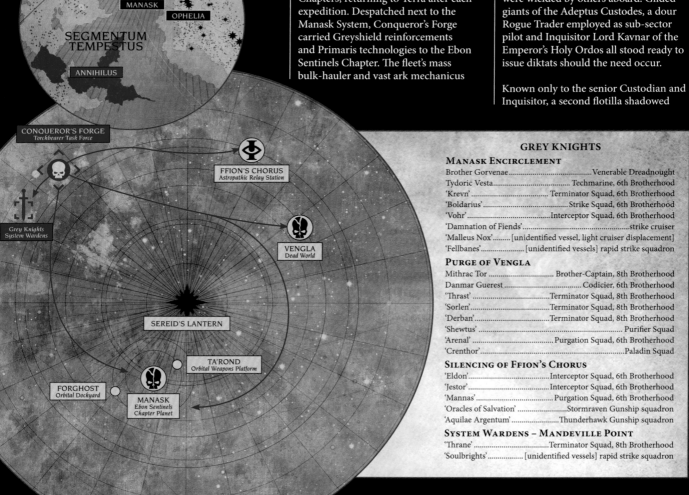

GREY KNIGHTS

MANASK ENCIRCLEMENT

Brother Gorvenae	Venerable Dreadnought
Tydoric Vesta	Techmarine, 6th Brotherhood
'Krevn'	Terminator Squad, 6th Brotherhood
'Boldarius'	Strike Squad, 6th Brotherhood
'Vohr'	Interceptor Squad, 6th Brotherhood
'Damnation of Fiends'	strike cruiser
'Malleus Nox'	[unidentified vessel, light cruiser displacement]
'Fellbanes'	[unidentified vessels] rapid strike squadron

PURGE OF VENGLA

Mithrac Tor	Brother-Captain, 8th Brotherhood
Danmar Guerest	Codicier, 6th Brotherhood
'Thrast'	Terminator Squad, 8th Brotherhood
'Sorlen'	Terminator Squad, 8th Brotherhood
'Derban'	Terminator Squad, 8th Brotherhood
'Shewtus'	Purifier Squad
'Arenal'	Purgation Squad, 6th Brotherhood
'Crenthor'	Paladin Squad

SILENCING OF FFION'S CHORUS

'Eldon'	Interceptor Squad, 6th Brotherhood
'Jestor'	Interceptor Squad, 6th Brotherhood
'Mannas'	Purgation Squad, 6th Brotherhood
'Oracles of Salvation'	Stormraven Gunship squadron
'Aquilae Argentum'	Thunderhawk Gunship squadron

SYSTEM WARDENS – MANDEVILLE POINT

'Thrane'	Terminator Squad, 8th Brotherhood
'Soulbrights'	[unidentified vessels] rapid strike squadron

It fills me with loathing and frustration to pen this missive. You have my initial report, sent when the Grey Knights' Edict of Forbiddance halted our progress. With the Emperor's Talons, I am enacting enquiries most thorough into the Greyshields we have aboard. There, we will find the weakness in their makeup that the Grey Knights are purging from their traitorous brothers. And what weakness! The system wardens whose 'guard' I have accepted have updated me. The Ebon Sentinels' Astropaths had been forced to be conduits for daemons. Warriors of the Adeptus Astartes have debased their Emperor-given gifts, pouring the warp into aspirants and inviting abominatus. With the Chapter's ships and means of escape crushed, the Grey Knights will prepare to unleash Exterminatus upon their home world.

By the authority of my seal, I pronounce the Ebon Sentinels Chapter of the Adeptus Astartes excommunicate traitoris.

– Inquisitor Lord Giorgius Kavnar, Ordo Malleus

Conqueror's Forge, unseen by their ships' sensors. The Prognosticars of Titan had seized damning omens from the immaterium of what Conqueror's Forge would encounter at Manask. The Ebon Sentinels were clinging to survival after punishing campaigns of loyal service. In their desperation to save off extinction they had heeded dark whispers that emanated from Vengla, a dead world of their home system. Promises of renewal, of swift and easy power led the Space Marines to employ the warp in their recruitment, and the Grey Knights had secretly accompanied Conqueror's Forge to purge the wayward Chapter.

Arriving in the system simultaneously with the task force, Grey Knights of the Rapiers and the Silver Blades spread out to isolate and destroy the Ebon Sentinels' orbital assets. Though much reduced in outright numbers, the traitor Chapter had the resources of an Adeptus Astartes home world with which to defend their new-found power. A splinter of the Grey Knights warded the system's fringe, issuing the Edict of Forbiddance via Inquisitor Kavnar to the Torchbearer Force. They remained at the Mandeville Point to ensure no Ebon Sentinel ships could escape and also to ensure none of the Torchbearer fleet strayed in-system.

An encirclement of rapid strike vessels, led by the strike cruiser *Damnation of*

Fighting at Ffion's Chorus, Justicar Gethnerin crushed traitor skulls with his Nemesis warding stave, Fellward, and fed his power through it to shield his squad.

Fiends, surrounded the Ebon Sentinels' home world and scuttled the remains of their fleet at the Forghost orbital docks. Teleporting Terminators and Strike Squads, meanwhile, attacked the linked weapons platforms of Ta'rond. Reinforced psychic communion from Ta'rond revealed the depths to which the Ebon Sentinels had sunk. There, meldings of Space Marines, possessed by daemons, mounted counter-attacks against the Grey Knights. At Ffion's Chorus – the system's astropathic relay – Terminators, Interceptors and Purgators deployed via gunships. There they destroyed the Ebon Sentinels' capacity to call for aid by eliminating surviving Astropaths to ensure any daemons had less chance to manifest.

Following the Prognosticars' strongest warning, the greater portion of the Grey Knights struck at Vengla, where they discovered an ancient daemonic presence imprisoned in its core. The beast's psychic influence, swollen by the Great Rift, seeped out beyond its million-year-old bonds, exploiting the Ebon Sentinels' desperation to survive and planting the seeds of their doom. Six squads led by Brother-Captain Tor of the Silver Blades deployed to enact a grand ritual of banishment. The daemon at Vengla's core responded by summoning a horde of warp-spawned vassals to its prison's surface, and with the debased traitors of the Ebon Sentinels fought back.

ARMOURY OF TITAN

The Grey Knights wield some of the finest and most advanced weapons in the Imperium. They are wrought with the arcane and the occult, with rituals that the uninitiated might fanatically condemn as sham spiritualism or vile witchery. The Grey Knights know with chilling intimacy the difference, and the need to employ every weapon in their unending war with the daemon.

THE DUTY OF MARS

Upon the inception of the Grey Knights, it was recognised that this necessarily secretive and embattled Chapter must have greater control over the production of its materiel. A pact was forged with the Tech-Priests of Mars, instigated with self-deleting protocols. Via arcanological means no longer known to the Adeptus Mechanicus, Mars' moon of Deimos was moved out of its Martian orbit and transferred to Titan.

Now, the heavily industrialised forges of Deimos thunder night and day to produce battle tanks, gunships, energy cells, combustion cores and far more,

including huge quantities of ammunition from bolt shells to the titanic ordnance required by starships. Deimos' manufactorums even produce some of the components for the Grey Knights' rare or unique weapons, though measures are taken to ensure the Tech-Priests cannot learn anything proscribed. These are delivered through cloistered means to the Grey Knights' armoury on Titan. It is here that the Chapter's Techmarines oversee their assembly and manage their ritual embellishment.

After his inculcation in the mysteries of the Tech-Priests' Cult of the Machine God, a Techmarine stands somewhat apart from his brothers. Few of the Cult's doctrines are compatible with those of the Grey Knights. Thus a Techmarine must balance the two sides of his nature: to serve the goals of the Grey Knights but according to the traditions of the Adeptus Mechanicus. The Chapter's goals override all else, however, and though adjustments they must make to holy constructs go against the tenets of Mars, Techmarines know the foe their Chapter faces in a way Tech-Priests never will. While steeped in aspects of their Cult, Techmarines owe no loyalty no Mars, and the Chapter Council relies upon them to guard against the Red Planet learning more than is good for it.

There are many esoteric technologies employed in the ember-lit and strangely shifting smoke of Titan's armoury. Psyk-out grenades are produced using a substance thought by some to be a by-product of the processes that sustain the Astronomican. Each of these explosives scatters a dense cloud of psi-refractive particles that can excruciate those who draw upon the warp's powers, or even fracture their fragile connection to the empyrean. That Grey Knights willingly carry to battle such devices so dangerous to themselves speaks of the selflessness by which they undertake their duty.

THE HOLY BOLTER

Bolt weapons are advanced and powerful firearms, whose difficulty to manufacture – and ferocious recoil – limit their use to the Imperium's martial elite. Bolts are small missiles: large bore, rapid firing, armour-piercing shells. Each houses a mass-reactive tip that triggers an explosive once the bolt has penetrated its target, inflicting crater-like wounds. Reliable and robust, they are endowed with a legendary status among the Space Marines with whom they are frequently associated, and the Grey Knights are no exception. The Sons of Titan commonly bear specialised vambrace-mounted storm bolters with twin barrels. They allow Grey Knights to fire streams of bolts at high volume via mind-impulse units and simultaneously wield their deadly Nemesis weapons with two hands. Larger bolt weapons are commonly mounted onto Razorback transports and the indomitable Land Raider battle tanks.

Elements of bolt technology are also employed in the ancient design of psycannons. Extremely rare, the secrets of their creation have been lost by a great number of forge worlds. The Grey Knights are among the few with the strength of mind and will to activate the silver-tipped and psychically charged munitions that psycannons fire.

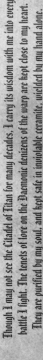

SOUL WEAPONS

In an entire Chapter of warp-harnessing warriors, psycannons are not the only empyrically imbued weapons. Most Grey Knights carry a force weapon attuned to their will. These Nemesis weapons are crafted by the Chapter's Techmarines; they are varied in form and unique in nature. From paired falchions and long-hafted halberds to immense daemon hammers and protective warding staves, each is an arcane forging of iron, silver, crystalline matrices and psychic circuitry. The ritual of dedication binds the weapon to its bearer, and through this link he channels his psychic might. The wielder's empyric strength makes ancient runes of daemon-slaying upon the weapon burn with a sanctified inner fire, adding to the power of the weapon's advanced disruptor field. After years of battle, a Grey Knight's force weapon retains part of his psyche imprinted upon its killing edge that will live on long after he has fallen, thereby making it an honoured ancestor weapon of the Chapter.

Among their unusual wargear are some whose technology the Chapter sources outside the Imperium or whose supply is arranged by segregated cells of the Ordo Malleus. The Grey Knights remain threateningly taciturn on such matters, though some Inquisitors believe that psilencers may originate down such unorthodox avenues. Psilencers and their kind do not possess physical triggering mechanisms. They are activated when their wielder sends a bolt of psychic force into the weapon's containment chamber. The Grey Knight's empyric power is channelled by a series of focusing crystals, and then unleashed as a punishing blast of azure psychic lances.

FEAT OF IRON

With grim practicality, Grey Knights acknowledge that the most monstrous warp-spawn – the Greater Daemons of Chaos – often wield far more power than a single battle-brother could hope to overcome. Once a Grey Knight's armour is locked into the command armature of a Nemesis Dreadknight, however, he is granted the strength and durability to match any daemonic lord. Only a very few Grey Knights have the mental fortitude and psychic subtlety to control the giant suit's mechanical limbs and devastating weaponry, while at the same time maintaining the psychic barrier of their Aegis. Those who do purge the unholy with blasts of psychically impregnated promethium from heavy incinerators or other powerful cannons, before smashing apart armoured foes and ragged mobs of lesser spawn with precision swings of their Nemesis great weapons.

Should a Grey Knight fall and his wounds prove too dire for the psychic chirurgery of the Chapter's Apothecaries to heal, he may yet serve at death's threshold within a Dreadnought. Deep inside the layers of adamantine alloy is a sarcophagus containing what remains of the fallen hero. Each is a warrior with centuries, sometimes millennia, of battlefield experience. They are kept alive by biomantic technology that connects them fully with the powerful robotic body they now inhabit. These honoured ancients are woken from stasis only in times of dire need. To fight one is to vainly attempt to defeat a great warrior of legend whose mortal frailties no longer hinder them.

A HIDDEN TAPESTRY

Upon the Grey Knights' sacred standards in the Hall of Champions, and within the locked pages of certain tomes that the Chapter holds, are described some of the most pivotal moments in the Imperium's history. These will never be lauded by thankful populaces and there are no statues to Grey Knights upon worlds they have saved – for there must be no witnesses.

The danger of unrestricted knowledge of the daemonic has been proven in the blood of entire worlds in which it was allowed to fester. Thus, not even the Grey Knights' greatest victories, upon worlds that have been thoroughly sanctified, can be known to Imperial citizens. Men and women who survive a daemonic incursion, even those who have impressed the Grey Knights with their stoic resolve in the face of mind-wrenching madness, are ruthlessly purged during extensive post-battle processing by the Ordo Malleus. The existence of such survivors is obviated by the Inquisition so completely that no record remains of certain regiments or ships' crews even being assigned to the system in question. It is likely that some forces recorded as being lost in the warp en route to their deployment actually reached their destination and fought with courage, only for the survivors to be rounded up, interrogated and executed. The Grey Knights are sometimes party to these purges as well, but the Ordo Malleus has resources and experience to conduct many by itself.

Particularly valued individuals such as warriors of other Space Marine Chapters and, occasionally, high-ranking commanders of the Astra Militarum or Navis Imperialis, are instead often psychically relieved of all memory of the battle. There have been occasions of resistance to such necessary mental excisions. At least one Chapter was forced to undertake an extended penitent crusade to the galactic rim rather than risk being branded Excommunicate Traitoris over their objections.

WAR IN THE WARP

Within the ancient warp storm known as Gheldrith's Eye, the Grey Knights uncovered a hidden ritual. Unfocused visions from the Augurium led a fleet of the 1st and 2nd Brotherhoods to discover an armada of Word Bearers Traitor Legion vessels inside the warp, positioned in an octagonal formation. A coven of Sorcerers and Dark Apostles were enacting a murderous ritual from within their ships. Already, warp-routes skirting Gheldrith's Eye were being perverted; the Geller fields of Imperial ships making these passages were weakened enough for lurking swarms of warp predators to tear them open and feast on their crews.

Though their own Geller fields were similarly weakened, the combined Aegis of the Grey Knights kept the circling

THE FIRST BATTLE FOR ARMAGEDDON

In the first half of the 41st Millennium, an unholy apocalypse engulfed the strategically vital planet of Armageddon. An armed rebellion began in Armageddon's manufactory-cities, as local warp storm activity increased. Planetary militias responded to brutally suppress these uprisings, but they were only the precursor to a greater threat. Its approach hidden by the warp storms, a space hulk, codenamed the *Devourer of Stars*, entered the system. Upon reaching the orbit of Armageddon itself, the huge hulk disgorged a horde of daemons, cultists, warp-spawn, possessed mutants and ancient Heretic Astartes of the World Eaters Legion, led by their ferocious Daemon Primarch, Angron.

The blood-drenched horde swept through Armageddon Prime, the western half of the planet's primary continent. Imperial reinforcements, including a major force of the Space Wolves Chapter, poured into the system. Millions lost their lives to the legions of daemonkind and warp-tainted berserkers in the first few weeks. The power of Angron and his horde were sustained by the roiling warp storms, however, and in a fickle lull in the tempests, the forces of Titan were able to launch the hammerblow of their attack. The defence

of Armageddon Secundus had held long enough for the arrival of Grey Knights from many brotherhoods. They teleported into the presence of Angron himself, battling the Daemon Primarch and the Bloodthirsters that fought with him. While other Imperial forces launched counter-attacks at Angron's horde, which had been weakened through the Grey Knights' overlapping Aegis, the Sons of Titan fought against Angron, his strikes cleaving apart entire squads of Terminators thanks to his immortal strength. Finally the Grey Knights were able to break his blade and banish his essence back to the warp, but the victory came at huge cost. A scant handful of Grey Knights survived the attack. From that pyrrhic triumph, however, strode warriors who would go on to forge even greater deeds – Arvann Stern, Vorth Mordrak and Garran Crowe among them.

The banishment of Angron was far from the end of Imperial losses. Alongside the Ordo Malleus, months were spent executing and mind-wiping billions more to eradicate knowledge of the invasion. Exacerbated by the Space Wolves' attempts to inhibit what they saw as dishonourable practices, even entire worlds were put to the sword simply to erase all mention of the battle.

daemons at bay. With their warp sight, the Grey Knights sensed the geometries of the ritual, otherwise invisible through the churning warp that enveloped them. They saw the psychic construction was almost complete, but could also see the nodes that could be unpicked to force the structure to unravel. The strike cruiser *Ceristor* led its sister ships in precision attacks that smashed through the gun decks of the Word Bearers' peripheral cruisers. Grey Knights made coordinated teleport strikes against bridge controls and enginariums. The ancient teleportariums were boosted by the psychic powers of the warriors so that none were scattered, even through the fluxing of the warp's local currents. The Chaos ships struggled to maintain their crucial positioning for the ritual. Their own gunnery inflicted minimal damage as it was buffeted by the energies of the halted ceremony. The Grey Knights disengaged as the ritual came apart and the warp's tides rushed in, tearing apart most of the Word Bearers' vessels.

THE RED TALON

Antraxes was a mining world famed throughout the Sudar Sub-sector for its rare bloodstone. When the Prognosticars foretold a great evil would arise there, a demi-brotherhood led by Brother-Captain Stern discovered the planet already in the grip of a rebellion. The Lord of Change, M'kachen, had spread an uprising from the Red Talon citadel, and the daemon had also tainted the bloodstone mines, binding warp nightmares into the rock. With its export, M'kachen's influence spread through the Sudar Sub-sector, sowing discord and mayhem as citizens wearing bloodstone tokens succumbed to possession.

Stern ordered half of his strike force to attack and destroy Antraxes' orbital shipyards, while he led the rest in a targeted strike at the Red Talon citadel. Teleporting into the midst of thousands of cultists enthralled to M'kachen, Stern and his warriors fought towards the daemon. He invoked the Liturgies of Banishment, duelling the Greater Daemon in a battle of wills as his brothers kept the surging cultists at bay with sweeps of their Nemesis blades and volleys of bolt-fire. Under Stern's psychic

onslaught, M'kachen's spells could not save it, and its mortal form burst apart in blue fire. The Grey Knights teleported clear as the flaming debris of the destroyed shipyards struck.

THE LION'S GATE INCURSION

The returned Primarch, Roboute Guilliman, had not been upon Terra long before the cataclysmic eruption of the Cicatrix Maledictum. Upon the Throneworld, the descending Blackness drove millions to insanity and rebellious cults arose in many of Terra's hive cities. Warp storms surrounding the planet split open and legions of Khornate daemons assaulted the Lion's Gate. This bastion at the heart of the Imperial Palace was

flanked by battleship-sized gun batteries, but alone they had no hope of prevailing. A demi-brotherhood of Grey Knights, despatched in haste to Terra, fought shoulder to shoulder with thousands of the Adeptus Custodes and countless more defenders. The Grey Knights' specialist knowledge, coordinated strikes and empyric powers helped stem the tide of eighty-eight cohorts of blood-drenched daemons. With the deployment of Sisters of Silence, the Grey Knights fought on with their superlative martial might even without their powers, stoically enduring the excruciating touch of the Null Maidens' psychic void. When the Lion's Gate was at last reinforced from other portions of the palace, the daemons were finally cast down and banished.

HERALDRY OF TITAN

The Grey Knights' millennia-long history is built upon a web of ancient traditions, vows of brotherhood and personal oaths. These sacred customs and doctrines are reflected in the weapons they use, the armour they wear and the heraldry they proudly bear.

Each Grey Knight's armour is an ancient relic drawn from the Chapter's armouries, and has often been worn by many warriors before him. Sometimes their names or deeds will be etched upon the plates of their armour, a preserved memory of their glory. More often, the artificer-crafted engravings are excerpts from the Liber Daemonica, the Canticle of Absolution, the Excrutiato Diabolus or any of countless other tracts.

The Chapter icon of a book speared through its spine by a blade emblazons their left pauldron and the armoured flanks of their battle tanks, gunships and even their sleek warships. Besides this, their unpainted armour bears a far more esoteric and individual appearance than those of other Space Marine Chapters. In traditional accents of red, black and white, warriors display their personal heraldries, often honoured with seals of sacred wax bearing vows of purgation or sanctity. Scrolls sealed in leather canisters, tomes of forbidden knowledge or fetishes made of honoured predecessors used in arcane rituals are carried alongside the most advanced technology the Imperium can create.

Grey Knight Personal Heraldry
Battle-brothers display their unique heraldry upon their oath shields. The simple designs represent their deeds, though to outsiders the meanings of these mysterious symbols are unknown. As a Grey Knight advances in rank he will add to his shield to reflect his elevated standing. For many Grey Knights, this is the only record of their actions.

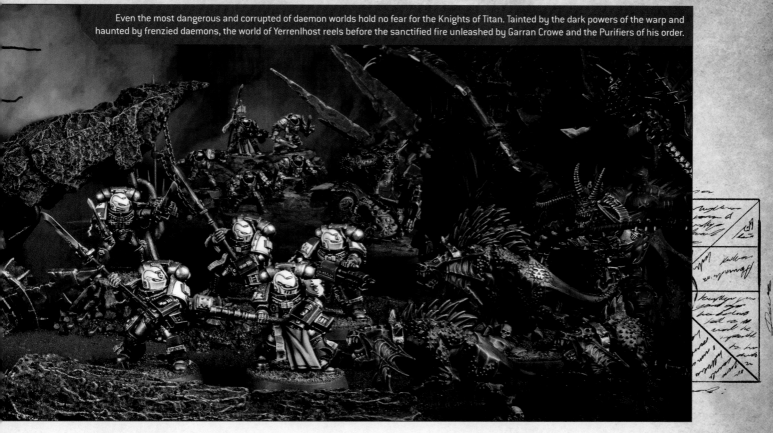

Even the most dangerous and corrupted of daemon worlds hold no fear for the Knights of Titan. Tainted by the dark powers of the warp and haunted by frenzied daemons, the world of Yerrenlhost reels before the sanctified fire unleashed by Garran Crowe and the Purifiers of his order.

FILE: 666M-AN - GREY KNIGHTS STRATEGIC DESIGNATIONS

Grey Knight with Nemesis force sword and storm bolter

Grey Knight Justicar with Nemesis force sword and storm bolter

Purgator with psycannon

Interceptor with incinerator

Brotherhood Terminator with Nemesis daemon hammer and storm bolter

Brotherhood Terminator with Nemesis force sword and psilencer

Terminator Justicar with Nemesis force halberd and storm bolter

In the shifting maze of the Nautiloid Palace on Forgantis, elite Paladins confront the orchestrator of the planet's descent into excess. Resisting the Greater Daemon's psychic siren song, the Paladins prepare a fragment of the creature's True Name to rip apart its corporeal form.

Purifier with Nemesis warding stave

Purifier with Nemesis falchions

Purifier with Nemesis daemon hammer

Knight of the Flame with Nemesis force sword

Esoteric Symbology
Each icon, from colour to positioning, has its own arcano-cryptic meaning within the Chapter. Skulls indicate the quelling of daemonic foes, and swords denote deeds that turned the tide of war. A stylised Imperial Aquila represents a great act of service to the Emperor, and is typically only worn by Grand Masters, Brother Captains and elite Paladins.

Paladin with Nemesis force sword
and incinerator

Paladin with Nemesis falchions
and storm bolter

The ruins of Hive Tertius still smoulder with empyric fire, its walls stained with the sooty imprints of its citizens. Into this inferno, the Order of Purifiers strike down the gibbering hellspawn that wrought such destruction, pitting soul flame and blessed promethium against warpfire.

Land Raider Crusader converted with items from Forge World upgrade sets

The once-fertile agri world of Plenaris has rotted away, its surface pierced by spurs of warpstuff and crawling with daemonkind. A lightning-fast aerial purgation by the 2nd Brotherhood is bolstered by the arrival of the Supreme Grand Master, Kaldor Draigo.

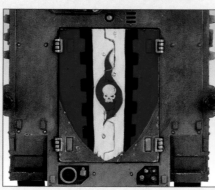

Grey Knight Vehicle Heraldry

Many armoured vehicles of the Grey Knights Chapter bear the personal heraldry of their commanding pilot, the warrior granted the right to display his arms upon its indomitable flanks. In the traditional red, black and white of the Chapter, some bear unifying colours and symbols that mark them as being part of a larger squadron or they may honour the deeds of those brothers carried within the safety of their hull. The stylised letter I of the Inquisition may mark a vehicle as having fought alongside the Emperor's daemon-hunting investigators, and the purity and belligerence of the vehicle's machine spirit can also be commemorated.

In the deep mine workings of Kappetar Majoris, a roiling cloud of burning gases illuminates the fierce battles waged unseen by the planet's surface populace. Castellan Garran Crowe leads his Purifiers to purge the blood-mad horrors that seek to eviscerate the world from within.

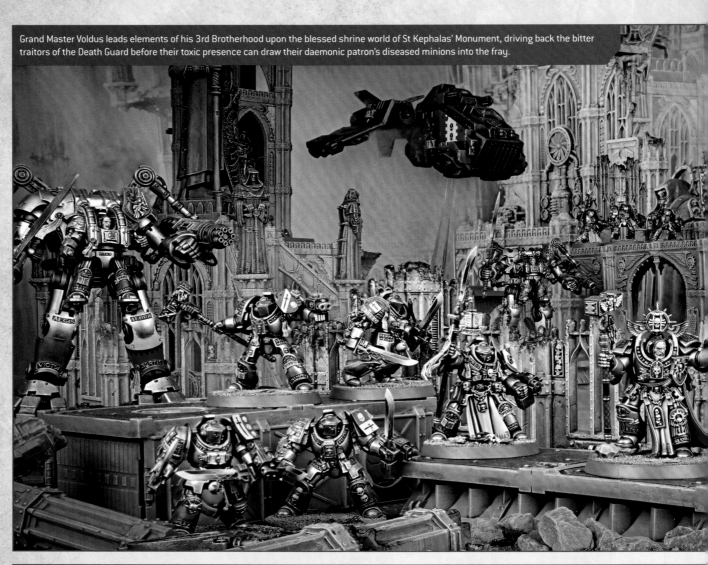

Grand Master Voldus leads elements of his 3rd Brotherhood upon the blessed shrine world of St Kephalas' Monument, driving back the bitter traitors of the Death Guard before their toxic presence can draw their daemonic patron's diseased minions into the fray.

As Champion of the Order of Purifiers, Garran Crowe embodies his brothers' sanctity and exemplifies their martial prowess. On the shadowy forge world of Tractis, he faced down the corpulent and noisome monstrosity Bo'rboryg, Crowe's swordsmanship and unyielding will flawless.

Grand Master in Nemesis Dreadknight with heavy incinerator, gatling psilencer and Nemesis greatsword. This model has been converted by the Warhammer 40,000 Army Painters to strike a suitably heroic pose.

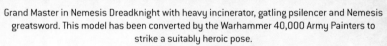

Castellan Crowe

Grand Master Voldus

THE RULES

Welcome to the rules section of *Codex: Grey Knights*. On the following pages you will find all the rules content you need to bring fire and destruction upon the foul denizens of the warp. Maybe you're inspired to dive straight into some open play games; maybe you want to forge your own tales of glory and infamy with narrative play; perhaps you can't wait to pit yourself against your opponents in nail-biting matched play contests; whichever appeals to you – even if it's a bit of all three – this section of your Codex provides a modular toolbox that allows you to get the most out of your collection.

Of course, there's no need to take it all in at once! Some of the content on the following pages, things like your army's datasheets and the rules for its weapons, will be useful no matter what kind of game you're playing. Others – such as your army's Stratagems, Warlord Traits and Relics – will become relevant once you start playing games with Battle-forged armies. Then there's content such as the Wisdom of the Prognosticars, allowing your mightiest champions to gain a measure of foresight about what they might face to give them an advantage on the battlefield, or the Masters of the Warp ability, allowing your warriors to manipulate the tides of warp energy to enhance their potential. In each case, you can include these new elements at your own pace; whether you're a brand new hobbyist playing your first few games or a veteran general ready to cause carnage, there's plenty here to provide countless hours of fresh and exciting gameplay.

You will find everything you need on the following pages to include these in your games of Warhammer 40,000, not to mention bespoke content for your Grey Knights Crusade force. Included in the latter is an exciting system allowing your Grey Knights characters to track down and banish their daemonic nemesis, that malevolent force that dogs them throughout their lifetime as one of the Emperor's elite daemon hunters. This content and the rest that you will find in this tome ensures that a Grey Knights Crusade force has a playstyle quite unlike any other, ensuring an array of unique tactical challenges in the battles to come.

BATTLE-FORGED RULES

DETACHMENT ABILITIES (PG 45)
Units in Grey Knights Detachments gain additional abilities to reflect how these elite daemon-hunters operate together and wage war on the battlefield, including The Aegis. You can find out more about Detachment abilities in the Battle-forged Armies section of the Warhammer 40,000 Core Book.

BROTHERHOOD OF PSYKERS (PG 45-53)
Grey Knights Detachments in your army can be from one of the brotherhoods of the Chapter. If they are, units in that Detachment will have access to unique rules that reflect the way those brotherhoods fight in the 41st Millennium.

WISDOM OF THE PROGNOSTICARS (PG 54-56)
Certain character models in your Grey Knights army can consult the Prognosticars before battle and gain valuable insights into the battle to come. This will grant them additional abilities or upgrades to use during the battle.

STRATAGEMS (PG 58-61)
Grey Knights armies have access to unique battlefield strategies and tactics that they can utilise to best their foes in any theatre of war; these are represented by the Stratagems in this section, which you can spend Command points on to use in your games. You can find out more about Stratagems and Command points in the Warhammer 40,000 Core Book.

ARMY RULES

RELICS (PG 62-63)
Grey Knights heroes can be equipped with powerful artefacts and venerated weapons called Relics of Titan; these Relics and the rules they bestow are described in this section.

DOMINUS AND SANCTIC DISCIPLINES (PG 64-65)
Many units in Grey Knights armies are psykers. They can be given psychic powers from either the Dominus or Sanctic disciplines. This represents the different arcane lore and talents available to these units. You can find out more about psychic powers in the Warhammer 40,000 Core Book.

LITANIES OF PURITY (PG 66)
On the battlefield, Chaplains recite rousing Litanies to inspire their comrades to feats of heroism on the battlefield. The list of different litanies that each Brotherhood Chaplain in your army can choose from can be found in this section.

WARLORD TRAITS (PG 67)
The Warlord of a Grey Knights army can have one of the traits presented in this section. These help to better reflect their individual combat and command style on the battlefield.

MATCHED PLAY RULES

CHAPTER APPROVED RULES (PG 68)
If you are playing a battle that instructs you to select secondary objectives, then you will be able to choose from the additional Grey Knights ones printed here. These represent the tactical and strategic goals unique to Grey Knights armies. You can find out more about selecting secondary objectives in many matched play mission packs, including the Eternal War mission pack found in the Warhammer 40,000 Core Book.

CRUSADE RULES

CRUSADE (PG 70-79)
Grey Knights have access to a host of additional rules that enhance your Crusade experience and further personalise your Crusade force. These include bespoke Requisitions, Agendas, Crusade Relics and Battle Tactics that help to reflect the fighting style of these elite daemon-hunters. Amongst the rules presented in this section are rules for creating a daemonic nemesis for your warriors – a nefarious foe to hunt down and banish in your games.

DATASHEETS

DATASHEETS (PG 80-103)
This section is essential to all Grey Knights players, regardless of preferred play style, containing as it does the datasheets for Grey Knights units. Each datasheet describes, among other things, the profiles of its models, the wargear they can be equipped with and the abilities they have. You can find out more about datasheets in the Warhammer 40,000 Core Book.

WARGEAR

WEAPON PROFILES (PG 104-107)
This section provides wargear lists referenced in the wargear options of certain Grey Knights datasheets, as well as profiles for all of the weapons that Grey Knights units can be equipped with.

POINTS

POINTS VALUES (PG 108-109)
If you are playing a game that uses points values, you can use the alphabetised lists in this section to determine the points value of each unit in your army. These values will be reviewed annually.

RULES REFERENCE

GLOSSARY (PG 110)
In this section you will find a glossary of rules terms used in this Codex. This is intended to work alongside the glossary found in the Warhammer 40,000 Core Book, and aid in resolving any complex rules interactions that may arise.

REFERENCE (PG 111)
Here you will find a bullet-pointed rules reference that summarises some common Grey Knights rules found in the Codex, to help remind you how they work at a glance during your games.

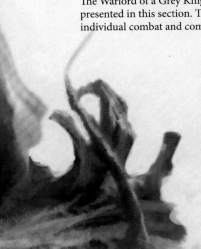

COMBAT PATROL

This Combat Patrol-sized collection is the perfect way to start a Grey Knights army, regardless of whether you want to play an open play game, forge an epic narrative with a Crusade army, or assemble a force to compete in a matched play mission. Created from the contents of the Combat Patrol: Grey Knights boxed set, this force can be used in a Battle-forged army, and in itself comprises a Patrol Detachment, as described in the Warhammer 40,000 Core Book.

On the battlefield, the Strike Squad and Terminators form a powerful core of troops. Each unit is not only a powerful force in the Psychic phase, but is also able to be armed with an array of melee and ranged weapons, allowing its models to deal a significant amount of damage despite their low numbers. The Terminators can also use their Teleport Strike ability to set up close to the enemy, ready to devastate them with heavy firepower and psychic powers before charging in to finish the survivors off in the Fight phase.

Leading these units is a Grey Knights Librarian. This Terminator-armoured warrior is a potent psyker, able to manifest multiple powers from the Dominus discipline each turn, as well as being incredibly resilient, and possessing a potent melee weapon. This commander can also be teleported into battle alongside your Terminators, allowing him to get to grips with the foe sooner.

Lastly, a Nemesis Dreadknight provides serious punch to the force. Able to be armed with an array of heavy ranged weapons, potent melee weapons, or a mix of the two, this powerful unit can be equipped to deal with enemy monsters and vehicles with blows from a Nemesis daemon greathammer, or burn away hordes of enemy troops with a heavy incinerator and gatling psilencer, all the while punishing the enemy with its psychic capabilities.

DETACHMENT ABILITIES

A **Grey Knights** Detachment is one that only includes models with the **Grey Knights** keyword (excluding models with the **Agent of the Imperium** or **Unaligned** keywords).

If your army is Battle-forged:

- **Grey Knights** Detachments gain the Brotherhood Command ability.
- **Grey Knights** units in **Grey Knights** Detachments gain The Aegis ability.
- **Grey Knights** Troops units in **Grey Knights** Detachments gain the Objective Secured ability (see the Warhammer 40,000 Core Book).

BROTHERHOOD COMMAND

The honour of leading the Grey Knights to war against the manifold threats of daemonkind falls to a brotherhood's commanding Grand Master and its honourable Brother-Captain.

- You can include a maximum of one **Grand Master** model and one **Brother-Captain** model in each Detachment in your army.
- Each **Grand Master** model in your army must be from a different brotherhood (pg 46-53).
- Each **Brother-Captain** model in your army must be from a different brotherhood.

THE AEGIS

The armour worn by the Grey Knights is inscribed with hexagrammic wards. In conjunction with the purity of spirit and psychic might of the wearer, they can resist otherworldly attacks.

- Each time a model in this unit would lose a wound as a result of a mortal wound, roll one D6: on a 5+, that wound is not lost.
- If this unit is a **Psyker**, add 1 to Deny the Witch tests taken for this unit.

BROTHERHOOD OF PSYKERS

If your army is Battle-forged, **<Brotherhood>** units in **Grey Knights** Detachments gain access to the following Brotherhood of Psykers rules, provided that every unit in that Detachment (excluding **Agent of The Imperium**, **Unaligned** and **Honoured Knight** units) is from the same brotherhood. Such a Detachment is referred to as a Brotherhood of Psykers Detachment.

PSYCHIC POWERS

Each brotherhood has an associated brotherhood psychic power. All **Grey Knights <Brotherhood> Psykers** in a Brotherhood of Psykers Detachment know the relevant brotherhood psychic power in addition to any other psychic powers they know.

WARLORD TRAITS

Each brotherhood has an associated brotherhood Warlord Trait. If a **Grey Knights <Brotherhood> Character** model gains a Warlord Trait, they can have the relevant brotherhood Warlord Trait instead of a Warlord Trait from page 67.

STRATAGEMS

Each brotherhood has an associated brotherhood Stratagem. If your army includes a Brotherhood of Psykers Detachment (excluding Auxiliary Support, Super-heavy Auxiliary and Fortification Network Detachments), then you will gain access to the relevant brotherhood Stratagem.

*Example: A Battle-forged army includes a **Grey Knights** Detachment in which every unit has the **Wardmakers** keyword. **Psyker** units in that Detachment gain the Projection of Purity psychic power, a **Character** in that Detachment that is given a Warlord Trait can instead be given the Loremaster trait, and you have access to the Masters of the Word Stratagem, and can spend CPs to use it.*

I see and feel every shining mind of my brothers, glittering through the tide of madness that embroils Mankind. The fierce corona of Menaril, the swirling vortex of Randellon and the pounding radiance of Thüboa... melded with the silver spear of Justicar Boreldus, we are an alloy of the Emperor's judgement.

BROTHERHOODS

'Beneath armoured tread shall we crush them, from the skies we will dominate them. No matter their number, no matter where they fester, we will find them and we will annihilate them.'

SWORDBEARERS

The 1st Brotherhood are experts in armoured assaults, and in coordinating the strikes of several elements to completely destroy prioritised targets. The brotherhood's epithet reflects both the blades of its warriors and its squadrons of tanks and gunships that slash at the enemy's heart, sheathed in sigil-enscribed armour plating.

MARKED FOR DEATH   2CP

Swordbearers – Battle Tactic Stratagem

The Swordbearers psychically upload the minutiae of the target's every move and position to their brothers, sealing the foes' doom.

Use this Stratagem at the start of your Shooting phase. Select one enemy unit within 12" of and visible to a SWORDBEARERS PSYKER unit from your army. Until the end of the phase, each time a friendly SWORDBEARERS unit makes a ranged attack against that enemy unit, add 1 to that attack's hit roll.

PSYCHIC POWER: EMPYRIC LODESTONE

The psyker attaches a subtle warp signature to the unsuspecting target, one that the psychic crews of the Swordbearers' battle tanks and gunships hone in on with punishing bombardments.

Malediction: *Empyric Lodestone* has a warp charge value of 7. If manifested, select one enemy unit within 18" of this PSYKER. Until the start of your next Psychic phase, each time a friendly SWORDBEARERS VEHICLE unit makes a ranged attack against that enemy unit, add 1 to that attack's wound roll. A unit can only be selected for this psychic power once per phase.

WARLORD TRAIT: RITES OF PROTECTION

This warlord has led countless armoured interdictions against the spawn of Chaos, and is adept at leading the crews of his powerful assets in rites that reinforce the sanctity of their Aegis.

If your WARLORD has this Warlord Trait, it can attempt to perform the following psychic action:

Rites of Protection (Psychic Action – Warp Charge 5): In your Psychic phase, this WARLORD can attempt to perform this psychic action. If completed, select one friendly SWORDBEARERS VEHICLE model within 12" of this WARLORD. Until the start of your next Psychic phase, that model has a 4+ invulnerable save.

BLADES OF VICTORY

The swiftest destruction of abominations ensures neither they nor any witnesses can escape, and the 2nd Brotherhood have perfected tactics not only of hard and fast strikes, but also of rapid redeployment. Caught by both the speed and strength of their strikes, from multiple attack angles, their enemies have no chance to avoid the Emperor's retribution.

RADIANT STRIKE   1CP

Blades of Victory – Strategic Ploy Stratagem

Psychic fire rimes the armour and blades of the 2nd Brotherhood's warriors as they charge at the foe, fanned by their battle fury. At the moment of contact, the empyric charge is unleashed in a blast of azure light.

Use this Stratagem in your Charge phase, when a **BLADES OF VICTORY CORE INFANTRY** unit from your army finishes a charge move. Select one enemy unit within Engagement Range of that **BLADES OF VICTORY** unit and roll one D6 for each model in that **BLADES OF VICTORY** unit that is within Engagement Range of that enemy unit. For each dice result that equals or exceeds that enemy unit's Toughness characteristic, it suffers 1 mortal wound.

PSYCHIC POWER: INESCAPABLE PURSUIT

Infusing his warriors with the temporal fluidity of the warp, the psyker grants their hunts the speed to ensure none can escape.

Blessing: *Inescapable Pursuit* has a warp charge value of 6. If manifested, until the start of your next Psychic phase, you can re-roll charge rolls made for this **PSYKER**'s unit.

WARLORD TRAIT: VANGUARD AGGRESSION

Forcing his enemies to react to his bold strategies, the warlord leads his battle-brothers in a swift attack, making straight for the enemy from an advance deployment.

After deployment, you can select one friendly **BLADES OF VICTORY CORE** unit within 9" of this Warlord. This **WARLORD** and the selected unit can each make a Normal Move of up to 6".

'There are no walls we cannot breach, no havens where the foul spawn of the warp can cower, safe from our fury. Where'er evil resides, we shall seek it out, and deliver unto it the Emperor's Justice.'

- Interceptor Gallius Tharon

BROTHERHOODS

> 'We are the warriors of the Grey Knights, armoured in Faith, shielded by Devotion and armed with Purity and Purpose. But greater even than these, we carry the light of the divine Emperor of Man into the dark places to purge the daemonic wherever it may be found.'
>
> – Brother-Captain Arvann Stern

WARDMAKERS

Possessed of a vast array of psychic knowledge, the 3rd Brotherhood are as adaptable in their ritual disciplines as in their martial skills. Few have the power to undo their potent psychic projections; even enemies fighting under fell influences find their masters' protection torn aside, their frailties uncovered by those from whom there are no secrets.

MASTERS OF THE WORD   1CP

Wardmakers – Epic Deed Stratagem

Senior adepts of the Wardmakers can plumb deep wells of empyric knowledge and even pool their talents across space and time, ensuring no foe is beyond them.

Use this Stratagem in your Command phase. Select one **WARDMAKERS CHARACTER** unit from your army. Select one psychic power from the Dominus discipline (pg 64) that model does not know to replace one of the psychic powers that it does.

PSYCHIC POWER: PROJECTION OF PURITY

The psyker projects his piercing gaze and purifying wards, cutting maleficent servants off from corruptive influence and revealing the true weaknesses of his foes.

Malediction: *Projection of Purity* has a warp charge value of 6. If manifested, select one enemy unit within 12" of this **PSYKER**. Until the start of your next Psychic phase, that unit is not affected by the aura abilities of models from its own army.

WARLORD TRAIT: LOREMASTER

The warlord is a psyker of prodigious strength, a master of his craft who has spent a lifetime learning the forbidden lore of the warp. Against such towering psychic power, there is little defence.

Each time a Psychic test is taken for this **WARLORD**, if the result of that test was an unmodified result of 8+ and it was greater than or equal to that power's warp charge value, your opponent cannot attempt to deny that power.

PRESCIENT BRETHREN

The battle-brothers of the 4th Brotherhood operate one step ahead of their enemies, instinctively channelling their martial and psychic skills to forge uncanny victories time after time. The Prescient Brethren have honed these skills over millennia, crafting temporal strategies that allow them to lie in wait for the enemy and avoid their clumsy traps in turn.

FORESIGHT — 1CP

Prescient Brethren – Battle Tactic Stratagem

Targeting their strikes a split second in advance of the enemy, the 4th Brotherhood predict their foes' movement, landing their shots and blows with preternatural accuracy.

Use this Stratagem in your Shooting phase, when a **PRESCIENT BRETHREN PSYKER** unit from your army is selected to shoot, or in the Fight phase, when a **PRESCIENT BRETHREN PSYKER** unit from your army fights. Until the end of the phase, each time a model in that unit makes an attack, re-roll a hit roll of 1 and re-roll a wound roll of 1.

PSYCHIC POWER: FATAL PRECOGNITION

The psyker fills his enemies' minds with horrific premonitions setting up loops of mental trepidation. Those who force themselves to forge onwards suffer massive cranial haemorrhages, their fear of the future warring with their will for control of their mind.

Malediction: *Fatal Precognition* has a warp charge value of 5. If manifested, select one enemy unit within 12" of this **PSYKER**. Until the start of your next Psychic phase, each time that enemy unit makes a Normal Move, Advances, Falls Back, or makes a charge move, roll one D6: on a 4-5, that enemy unit suffers D3 mortal wounds; on a 6, that enemy unit suffers 3 mortal wounds. A unit can only be selected for this psychic power once per phase.

WARLORD TRAIT: DIVINATION

This warlord can follow the skeins of future events, using his psychic gifts to filter the myriad possible outcomes before him and using the tactical insight he gains to sow his enemies' destruction.

If your **WARLORD** has this Warlord Trait, it can attempt to perform the following psychic action:

Divination (Psychic Action – Warp Charge 6): In your Psychic phase, this **WARLORD** can attempt to perform this psychic action. If completed, you gain 1CP.

'The daemon thinks itself clever, the daemon thinks itself swift. It believes it can outwit us, outmanoeuvre us and outdo us using every manner of trick and ploy. It is wrong. Our minds see past it all. Our minds see its plans and its weaknesses. We shall be its undoing.'

BROTHERHOODS

'We are sworn to fight for the Emperor unto death. By our means do our brothers fight even beyond death, for such is not a barrier to immortal duty. We are sworn to never waver in our task nor cease our wars. By what we preserve do we ensure we will stand against the daemon forever.'

PRESERVERS

Often fighting alongside many of the Chapter's most ancient and revered warriors, the 5th Brotherhood have perfected tactics around the imposing and inspiring presence of Dreadnoughts. The Preservers not only safeguard the knowledge and technology Dreadnoughts represent, they will also lay down their lives to deny any threats to their honour.

CHARGE OF THE ANCIENTS — 1CP

Preservers – Requisition Stratagem

Some Dreadnought chassis of the 5th Brotherhood have been maintained for millennia. Their ancient but singularly advanced servos enable those interred within to unleash their full fury.

Use this Stratagem before the battle, when you muster your army. Select one **PRESERVERS DREADNOUGHT** model from your army.

- That model has a Move characteristic of 8".
- You can re-roll charge rolls made for that model.
- Each time that model fights, if it made a charge move this turn, then until that fight is resolved, add 1 to the Damage characteristic of melee weapons that model is equipped with.

You can only use this Stratagem once, unless you are playing an Onslaught battle (in which case, you can use this Stratagem twice, on two different **PRESERVERS DREADNOUGHT** models from your army).

PSYCHIC POWER: AEGIS ETERNAL

The psyker weaves a coruscating aurora of psychic power into his allies' warding sigils, causing them to flare with protective power.

Blessing: *Aegis Eternal* has a warp charge value of 6. If manifested, until the start of your next Psychic phase, each time a model in this **PSYKER**'s unit would lose a wound, roll one D6: on a 6, that wound is not lost. While this **PSYKER**'s unit is within 3" of a friendly **GREY KNIGHTS APOTHECARY**, if this **PSYKER**'s unit is **INFANTRY**, that wound is not lost on a 5+ instead.

WARLORD TRAIT: RADIANT EXEMPLAR

This warlord is a warden of ancient secrets and a guardian of both the Chapter's past and future, his humility and willingness to inflict any sanction necessary in their defence an inspiration to all.

Add 3" to the range of this **WARLORD**'s aura abilities (to a maximum of 12").

RAPIERS

Masters of achieving victories against overwhelming forces with the precise application of sanctified power, the 6th Brotherhood quickly identify the fulcrums upon which the enemy's power hinges. Speed and the overpowering application of strength at the right point in time and space can topple the most far-reaching of daemonic schemes.

DEADLY EFFICACY   1CP

Rapiers – Battle Tactic Stratagem

The 6th Brotherhood's weapon masters teach that every blow counts. With matchless efficiency, economical attacks can parry, slash and pierce in a single strike.

Use this Stratagem in the Fight phase when a **RAPIERS** unit from your army is selected to fight. Until the end of the phase, each time a model in that unit makes a melee attack, an unmodified hit roll of 6 scores 1 additional hit.

PSYCHIC POWER: SYMPHONIC STRIKE

The psyker empowers his allies with a psychic sharpening of their senses, enabling them to attack in a flurry of coordinated blows that orchestrate their foes' downfall with faultless efficiency.

Blessing: *Symphonic Strike* has a warp charge value of 6. If manifested, until the start of your next Psychic phase, add 1 to the Attacks characteristic of models in this **PSYKER**'s unit.

WARLORD TRAIT: INESCAPABLE WRATH

This warlord strikes like a silver lance of lightning. By focusing his powers upon a pivotal moment, he connects himself via a tether of inevitability to his enemies. Drawn by the tether, he bears down upon them with incredible speed, ensuring none escape his wrath.

This **WARLORD** is eligible to declare a charge with even if they Advanced this turn.

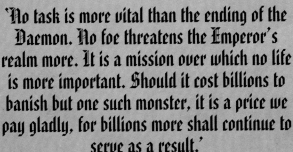

'No task is more vital than the ending of the Daemon. No foe threatens the Emperor's realm more. It is a mission over which no life is more important. Should it cost billions to banish but one such monster, it is a price we pay gladly, for billions more shall continue to serve as a result.'

BROTHERHOODS

'We do not stand alone. Though none can stand against the powers of the empyrean as we can, others serve as our eyes and ears. We pay them heed so we can make the daemon pay for every incursion, every infiltration and every invasion.'

EXACTORS

Specialists in mutually supportive tactics, the 7th Brotherhood ensures no element of their force is wasted or isolated. From coordinated strikes alongside Imperial elements supplied by the Ordo Malleus to the iron-hard bonds between their battle-brothers, the Exactors face the daemonic threat as inspiring guardians of Humanity.

SANCTIC GUARDIANS   1CP

Exactors – Strategic Ploy Stratagem

The Exactors embody the role of stern protectors, plunging into the fray to ensure no one faces the horrors of the galaxy alone.

Use this Stratagem in the Heroic Interventions step of your opponent's Charge phase. Select one **EXACTORS** unit from your army that is not within Engagement Range of any enemy units. Until the end of the phase, that unit can perform a Heroic Intervention as if it were a **CHARACTER**.

PSYCHIC POWER: FIRES OF COVENANT

Drawing upon his pledges of duty and the bonds of his brotherhood, the psyker releases a fiery conflagration of death.

Witchfire: *Fires of Covenant* has a warp charge value of 5. If manifested, select one enemy unit within Engagement Range of this **PSYKER**'s unit. Roll one D6 for each model in that enemy unit: for each roll of 4+, that enemy unit suffers 1 mortal wound (if the psyker manifesting this power has the Psychic Epitome Warlord Trait (pg 67), the enemy unit suffers 1 additional mortal wound after all these dice rolls have been made). Each unit can only be selected for this psychic power once per turn.

WARLORD TRAIT:
OATH OF WITNESS (AURA)

The warlord has witnessed the true cost of the corruption of Chaos among the vast throng of Humanity countless times. With a sacred vow of unquenchable valour made before his warriors, his determined presence is an illuminating beacon of hope.

- Add 1 to this **WARLORD**'s Leadership characteristic.
- While a friendly **EXACTORS CORE** unit is within 6" of this **WARLORD**, Morale tests taken for that unit are automatically passed.

SILVER BLADES

The 8th Brotherhood are exemplars of studied excellence and versatile tactics. Their resilient and adaptable strategies ensure they can respond swiftly to the frenetic and illogical machinations of their daemonic adversaries. Their extensive training, beyond that of other brotherhoods, allows them to undertake rapid changes in doctrine.

ADAPTIVE EXCORIATION   1CP

Silver Blades – Strategic Ploy Stratagem

Countless prideful enemies have been cut down by the Silver Blades' blistering firepower, having instantly turned an apparent withdrawal into retributive furore.

Use this Stratagem in your Movement phase, when a **Silver Blades Core** unit from your army Falls Back. That unit is still eligible to shoot this turn even though it Fell Back.

PSYCHIC POWER: TEMPORAL ACCURACY

The psyker reaches for the time-warping power of the immaterium, granting his battle-brothers the speed and foresight to target enemies even in the chaos and confusion of melee.

Blessing: *Temporal Accuracy* has a warp charge value of 5. If manifested, until the start of your next Psychic phase, all storm bolters, master-crafted storm bolters, and Relics that replace either of these weapons, that models in this **Psyker**'s unit are equipped with are treated as being Pistol 4 weapons with a range characteristic of 12".

WARLORD TRAIT: MARTIAL PERFECTION

Having undertaken the rigorous trials of initiation many times, this warlord is a master of many forms of combat and his lethal skill in close quarters has lined the Hall of Champions with countless trophies.

- At the start of the Fight phase, if this **Warlord** is within Engagement Range of any enemy units, it can fight first that phase.
- Each time this **Warlord** makes a melee attack, you can re-roll the hit roll.

'To us is entrusted the future. Upon our shoulders the burden of ensuring the strength and skill of the Chapter rests. Perfection is our one and only standard. In every manner of war must we be sublime, for the daemon's artifice is infinite and we face it down wherever it rears its head.'

WISDOM OF THE PROGNOSTICARS

If your army is Battle-forged and includes any GREY KNIGHTS Detachments (excluding Auxiliary Support, Super-heavy Auxiliary and Fortification Network Detachments), then when you are mustering your army, you can upgrade any of the GREY KNIGHTS CHARACTER models in your army by giving them either a Vision of the Augurium or a Gift of the Prescient, chosen from those presented here. Each time you do so, that CHARACTER model's Power Rating is increased by the amount shown in the relevant table below. If you are playing a matched play game, or a game that uses a points limit, then the points value of that model is also increased by the amount shown on the same table. Make a note on your army roster each time you give a CHARACTER model one of these upgrades.

Named characters cannot be given any of these upgrades. Each CHARACTER model cannot have more than one of these upgrades, and an army (or a Crusade force) cannot include the same upgrade more than once. Visions of the Augurium and Gifts of the Prescient are not considered to be Relics for any rules purposes – this means a CHARACTER model can be equipped with both a Relic and one of these upgrades.

A Crusade force cannot start with any CHARACTERS having a Vision of the Augurium or a Gift of the Prescient – to do so you must use the Consult the Prognosticars Requisition (pg 72).

VISIONS OF THE AUGURIUM

VISION	POWER	POINTS
Augury of Aggression	+1	+20
Heroism's Favour	+1	+15
A Noble Death	+1	+20
Omen of Incursion	+2	+30
Presaged Paralysis	+1	+15
Foretelling of Locus	+2	+30

GIFTS OF THE PRESCIENT

GIFT	POWER	POINTS
True Name Shard	+1	+10
Temporal Bombs	+1	+15
Servant of the Throne	+1	+20
Deluminator of Majesty	+1	+15
Gem of Inoktu	+1	+15
Severance Bolt	+2	+30

VISIONS OF THE AUGURIUM

Within the silver pinnacle of the Augurium, the Prognosticars have foreseen key events of the battle ahead. One who seeks their wisdom may be granted valuable tactical foresight. When the presaged moment comes, they will already be one step ahead of their opponents.

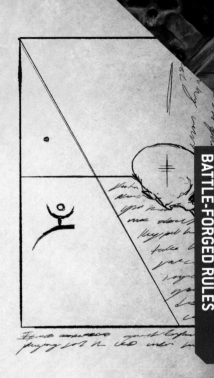

AUGURY OF AGGRESSION

The vision speaks of onrushing assailants filled with murderous malice. The warning's recipient has already prepared his response and the enemy appears exactly as predicted, right in the Grey Knights' gun sights.

Once per battle, when a friendly **GREY KNIGHTS CORE** or **GREY KNIGHTS CHARACTER** unit within 12" of this model is selected to fire Overwatch, this model can experience this vision. If it does, then until the end of the phase, each time a model in that unit makes an Overwatch attack, a hit is scored on an unmodified roll of 4+.

HEROISM'S FAVOUR

The enemy's brazen manoeuvre, as revealed by the vision, is an opportunity for the recipient's brethren to launch a valorous counter-punch.

Once per battle, at the end of your opponent's Charge phase, you can select one friendly **GREY KNIGHTS CORE** unit within 12" of this model. That unit can perform a Heroic Intervention as if it were a **CHARACTER**.

A NOBLE DEATH

The vision's recipient is warned of their fated demise, but such is his determination to meet it with strength that his brothers are inspired to match his nobility. With such fortitude, maybe the path of the future can be changed and death, at that point, shunned.

Once per battle, in your Command phase, this model can experience this vision. If it does, until the start of your next Command phase, it gains the following ability: '**A Noble Death (Aura):** While a friendly **GREY KNIGHTS CORE** or **GREY KNIGHTS CHARACTER** unit is within 6" of this model, it gains the Objective Secured ability (see the Warhammer 40,000 Core Book) and can Set to Defend. If a model in that unit already has the Objective Secured ability, that model counts as one additional model when determining control of an objective marker.'

OMEN OF INCURSION

The vision foretells of a sudden and violent strike by previously unseen foes. Thus forewarned, the recipient lays his plans and a greeting of devastating firepower awaits the attackers.

Once per battle, at the end of the Reinforcements step of your opponent's Movement phase, this model can experience this vision. If it does, select one **GREY KNIGHTS CORE** or **GREY KNIGHTS CHARACTER** unit from your army that is not within Engagement Range of any enemy units. That unit can shoot as if it were your Shooting phase, but its models can only target a single eligible enemy unit that was set up as Reinforcements this turn and that is within 12" of their unit when doing so.

PRESAGED PARALYSIS

In this moment are the enemy blighted by inaction and tormented by indecision, so showed the vision. They are ripe for an ambush long prepared for this fated instant.

Once per battle, at the start of your Charge phase, if this model is on the battlefield, you can select one enemy unit on the battlefield. Until the end of the phase, that unit cannot fire Overwatch or Set to Defend.

FORETELLING OF LOCUS

The vision signified the hidden ways of the battlefield and the enemy's ploys, granting the recipient a prophetic situational awareness which aids his brothers in their strategic disposition.

After both players have deployed their armies, select up to three **GREY KNIGHTS CORE** units from your army and redeploy them. If the mission uses the Strategic Reserves rules, any of those units can be placed into Strategic Reserves without having to spend any additional CPs, regardless of how many units are already in Strategic Reserves. If both players have abilities that redeploy units, roll off; the winner chooses who redeploys their units first.

GIFTS OF THE PRESCIENT

The Prognosticars of the Grey Knights may grant their wisdom via the bequest of an artefact. Their auguries sometimes reveal a moment of pivotal import. Then, and only then, will their gift fulfil its purpose, for each is a specialised article crafted to be employed at a certain juncture foreseen from the Citadel of Titan.

TRUE NAME SHARD

At the moment the warp-spawn overreaches, the fragment of its True Name on this shade-film scroll is read aloud and driven by the bearer's psychic will into its daemonic flesh. The scroll will crumble, but its power staggers even one of the Conclave Diabolus.

Once per battle, at the start of the Fight phase, you can select one enemy **DAEMON** unit within 6" of the bearer. That unit is not eligible to fight this phase until after all eligible units from your army have done so.

TEMPORAL BOMBS

Havens of the unclean and sites of purity are sanctified with these soul-reactive devices. Seeded in a hallowed moment within the floes of the churning warp, they transition into realspace without causing a breach, using the power of that shift to detonate.

Before the battle, select one Area Terrain feature that is not within your opponent's deployment zone and note it down secretly on your army roster. The first time an enemy unit starts or ends a move on or within that terrain feature, reveal your choice and roll one D6: on a 2+, that enemy unit suffers D3 mortal wounds.

SERVANT OF THE THRONE

Bound into the warrior's vambrace is the psychic death throe of one sacrificed to the workings of the Golden Throne. Held in empyric suspension, their radiance shines out in the prophesied instant, turning aside blows with an aura of unsullied duty.

Once per battle, when the bearer is selected as the target of an attack, it can use this gift. If it does, then until the end of the turn, the bearer has a 3+ invulnerable save.

DELUMINATOR OF MAJESTY

The dark radiance of the daemon is foreseen, its influence spilling from its flesh in waves. Inscribed with six hundred and sixty-six truths about its paltry non-existence, when this bolt explodes the daemon's abominable veneer of grandeur is shredded, revealing it for the twisted pretender it truly is.

When you give a model this gift, select one bolt weapon (pg 104) that model is equipped with. Once per battle, when the bearer shoots with that weapon, you can choose for it to fire a Deluminator of Majesty bolt.

If you do, you can only make one attack with that weapon, but if it scores a hit against a **DAEMON** unit, until the start of your next Shooting phase, that unit loses any aura abilities it has, in addition to any normal damage.

GEM OF INOKTU

One of the fabled gems that fall as rain deep in the immaterial layers of the gas giant Inoktu, this small jewel flares brightly at the appointed hour. Used as a prism of focus, the bearer can channel incredible power through it before its time is spent and it becomes as inert and opaque as a lifeless eye.

Once per battle, when the bearer is selected to manifest psychic powers, you can use this gift. If you do, then until the end of the phase, each time the bearer attempts to manifest a psychic power from the Dominus discipline (pg 64), add 2 to that attempt's Psychic test.

SEVERANCE BOLT

An enemy of the Chapter is pinpointed to this battle, a foe the Prognosticars have hunted through countless visions. This Severance Bolt – as unique as all others – was prepared long ago, awaiting this moment. Steeped in psychic power, the enemy's past and future misdeeds chanted over it, this silver-tipped bolt will hone in on its prey's warp signature to the exclusion of all others.

When you give a model this gift, select one bolt weapon (pg 104) that model is equipped with. Before the battle, select one enemy **CHARACTER** unit. Once per battle, when the bearer shoots with that weapon, you can choose for it to fire a Severance Bolt.

If you do, you can only make one attack with that weapon, but when selecting a target, you can ignore the Look Out, Sir rule so long as you select that **CHARACTER** unit as the target. When making an attack with a Severance Bolt against that **CHARACTER** unit, if it successfully hits the target:

- The target suffers D3 mortal wounds and the attack sequence ends.
- If the target is a **PSYKER**, roll 3D6; if the result exceeds the target's Leadership characteristic, randomly select one psychic power that it knows. That **PSYKER** cannot use that psychic power for the rest of the battle.

STRATAGEMS

If your army includes any **GREY KNIGHTS** Detachments (excluding Auxiliary Support, Super-heavy Auxiliary and Fortification Network Detachments), you have access to these Stratagems, and can spend CPs to use them.

PSYCHIC CHANNELLING   1CP

Grey Knights – Battle Tactic Stratagem

Even in the midst of ferocious combat, a Grey Knight can unfetter the full potential of their finely crafted psychic talents.

Use this Stratagem in your Psychic phase, when a **GREY KNIGHTS PSYKER** unit from your army is selected to manifest psychic powers. Until the end of the phase, each time a Psychic test is taken for that unit, roll one additional D6 and discard one of the dice.

PSYCHIC ONSLAUGHT   1CP

Grey Knights – Battle Tactic Stratagem

Psi weaponry can be used to channel a battle-brother's fury. The wrath of Titan is a cold and calm detestation that few can weather.

Use this Stratagem in your Shooting phase, when a **GREY KNIGHTS PSYKER** unit from your army is selected to shoot. Until the end of the phase, each time a model in that unit makes a ranged attack with a psi weapon (pg 104), add 1 to the Strength characteristic of that attack and improve the Armour Penetration characteristic of that attack by 1.

THE STEEL HEART   1CP

Grey Knights – Battle Tactic Stratagem

Terminator-armoured warriors are the steel heart of the Grey Knights' strikes. They exemplify the Chapter's qualities as truly potent combatants.

Use this Stratagem in your Fight phase, when a **GREY KNIGHTS TERMINATOR** unit from your army is selected to fight. Until the end of the phase, each time a model in that unit makes a melee attack, add 1 to that attack's hit roll.

DEATH FROM THE WARP   1CP

Grey Knights – Battle Tactic Stratagem

Utilising their warp-attuned senses during the timeless instant of teleportation, Grey Knights know exactly where the enemy are before they arrive. They emerge from the blinding flare of warp energies already firing.

Use this Stratagem in your Shooting phase, when a **GREY KNIGHTS PSYKER** unit from your army shoots. Until the end of the phase, each time a model in that unit makes a ranged attack, if that unit was set up on the battlefield using the Teleport Strike ability this turn, add 1 to that attack's hit roll.

POWERFUL ADEPT   1CP

Grey Knights – Battle Tactic Stratagem

Battle-brothers of the Grey Knights are masters of the arcane, capable of extending their powers through ritualistic projection.

Use this Stratagem in your Psychic phase, when a **GREY KNIGHTS PSYKER** unit from your army is selected to manifest psychic powers. Until the end of the phase, each time a psychic power is manifested by that unit, increase the range of that psychic power by 6".

SANCTIFIED KILL ZONE   2CP

Grey Knights – Battle Tactic Stratagem

The sheer volume of eviscerating firepower unleashed by Purgation Squads at close range forms an extreme kill zone in which there is little chance of survival.

Use this Stratagem in your Shooting phase, when a **PURGATION SQUAD** unit from your army is selected to shoot. Until the end of the phase, each time a ranged attack made by a model in that unit targets an enemy unit within half range, add 1 to that attack's wound roll.

FINAL JUSTICE   2CP

Grey Knights – Epic Deed Stratagem

Even imminent death will not prevent a Grey Knight from enacting his final justice upon the enemies of the Emperor.

Use this Stratagem in the Fight phase, when a **GREY KNIGHTS CHARACTER** model (excluding **CASTELLAN CROWE**) from your army that has not already been selected to fight this phase is destroyed. Do not remove that model from play – it can fight after the attacking model's unit has finished making attacks. After resolving the destroyed model's attacks, it is then removed.

SHADOW OF UNDYING LEGENDS   1CP

Grey Knights – Epic Deed Stratagem

Grey Knights Dreadnoughts are a link to the Chapter's glorious past. They are living legends, whose mere presence inspires those battle-brothers who fight in their shadow to great deeds.

Use this Stratagem in your Command phase. Select one **GREY KNIGHTS DREADNOUGHT** model from your army. Until the start of your next Command phase, that model gains either the Rites of Battle ability or the Tactical Precision ability, as shown below:

- **Rites of Battle (Aura):** While a friendly **GREY KNIGHTS CORE** unit is within 6" of this model, each time a model in that unit makes an attack, re-roll a hit roll of 1.
- **Tactical Precision (Aura):** While a friendly **GREY KNIGHTS CORE** unit is within 6" of this model, each time a model in that unit makes an attack, re-roll a wound roll of 1.

PURITY OF THE MACHINE SPIRIT — 2CP

Grey Knights – Epic Deed Stratagem

The most ancient and pure of the Grey Knights' machine spirits are known to continue the fight with an inviolable sense of duty.

Use this Stratagem in your Command phase. Select one **Grey Knights Machine Spirit** model from your army. Until the start of your next Command phase, that model is considered to have its full wounds remaining for the purposes of determining what characteristics on its profile to use.

EMPYRIC DECLAMATION — 2CP

Grey Knights – Epic Deed Stratagem

The Chaplain drives the force of his oratory with psychic fervour, ensuring his fiery inspiration is felt within his brothers' very souls.

Use this Stratagem at the start of any of your phases. Select one **Brotherhood Chaplain** unit from your army that has not recited a litany since the start of your last Command phase. That model can recite one litany that has not already been recited by a friendly model since the start of your last Command phase. That litany is automatically inspiring (do not roll) and takes effect until the start of your next Command phase.

CHIRURGIC RESURRECTION — 1CP

Grey Knights – Epic Deed Stratagem

With sanctified narthecium, blessed unguents and empyric ritual, Apothecaries swiftly return wounded brothers to the endless war.

Use this Stratagem at the end of your Movement phase. Select one **Grey Knights Apothecary** unit from your army and then select one friendly **Grey Knights Infantry** unit that is not at its Starting Strength and is within 3" of that **Apothecary**. One of the selected unit's destroyed models is returned to its unit with its full wounds remaining.

PSYCHIC LOCUS — 2CP

Grey Knights – Epic Deed Stratagem

Brother-Captains maintain constant psychic contact with their warriors, focusing and strengthening their powers.

Use this Stratagem at the start of your Psychic phase. Select one **Brother-Captain** model from your army. Until the end of the phase, that model gains the following ability: 'Psychic Locus (Aura): While a friendly **<Brotherhood> Psyker** unit is within 6" of this model, add 1 to Psychic tests taken for that unit.'

FINEST HOUR — 1CP

Grey Knights – Epic Deed Stratagem

It is in the darkest times that the disciplined fury of the Grey Knights burns its brightest.

Use this Stratagem at the start of any phase. Select one **Grey Knights Character** unit from your army. Until the end of the turn, add 3" to the range of that unit's aura abilities (to a maximum of 12").

THUNDEROUS STRIDE — 1CP

Grey Knights – Epic Deed Stratagem

Capable of the subtlety and finesse of a blade, Dreadknight suits can also be wielded with the force of a descending hammerblow.

Use this Stratagem in your Charge phase, when a **Dreadknight** model from your army finishes a charge move. Select one enemy unit within Engagement Range of that model, and roll one D6: on a 2-5, that enemy unit suffers D3 mortal wounds; on a 6, that enemy unit suffers 3 mortal wounds.

ARMOURY OF TITAN — 1CP

Grey Knights – Requisition Stratagem

The Chapter's most sacred artefacts lie in hallowed vaults deep within the Citadel of Titan, guarded by unsleeping sentinels.

Use this Stratagem before the battle, when you are mustering your army, if your **Warlord** has the **Grey Knights** keyword. Select one **Grey Knights Character** model from your army and give them one Relic of Titan (this must be a Relic they could have). Each Relic in your army must be unique, and you cannot use this Stratagem to give a model two Relics. You can only use this Stratagem once, unless you are playing a Strike Force battle (in which case, you can use this Stratagem twice) or an Onslaught battle (in which case, you can use this Stratagem three times).

EXEMPLAR OF THE SILVERED HOST — 1CP

Grey Knights – Requisition Stratagem

To be ordained as a Grey Knight is to succeed where millions are deemed unworthy, and some of their champions stand higher still.

Use this Stratagem after nominating a **Grey Knights Character** model that is not a named character to be your **Warlord**. Generate one additional Warlord Trait for them; this must be from the Grey Knights Warlord Traits table (pg 67). Each Warlord Trait in your army must be unique (if randomly generated, re-roll duplicate results). You can only use this Stratagem once.

SHIELD OF HUMANITY — 1CP

Grey Knights – Requisition Stratagem

Between Humanity and the threat foreseen by the Emperor stand heroes whose names are lauded only in the Hall of Champions.

Use this Stratagem before the battle, when you are mustering your army, if your **Warlord** has the **Grey Knights** keyword. Select one **Grey Knights Character** from your army and determine one Warlord Trait for that model (this must be a Warlord Trait they could have); that model is only regarded as your **Warlord** for the purposes of that Warlord Trait. Each Warlord Trait in your army must be unique (if randomly generated, re-roll duplicate results), and you cannot use this Stratagem to give a model two Warlord Traits. You can only use this Stratagem once, unless you are playing a Strike Force battle (in which case, you can use this Stratagem twice) or an Onslaught battle (in which case, you can use this Stratagem three times).

Though he may lead a strike force to battle, a Chaplain's primary duty is to the spiritual fortitude of the Brotherhood he fights amongst. With fiery oratory, he sharpens their specialised rituals and projects his canticles through their psychic communion.

ENDOWMENT IN EXTREMIS   1CP

Grey Knights – Requisition Stratagem

At the Prognosticars' urging, Titan's reliquaries are opened and proven veterans are entrusted with artefacts of ancient power.

Use this Stratagem before the battle. Select one **GREY KNIGHTS** model from your army that has one of the following in their profile: 'Justicar'; 'Paragon'; 'Knight of the Flame'. That model can have one of the following Relics of Titan, even though they are not a **CHARACTER**: Domina Liber Daemonica; Sanctic Shard; Augurium Scrolls; Stave of Supremacy (pg 62-63). All of the Relics your army includes must be different and be given to different models.

MENTAL FOCUS   1CP

Grey Knights – Strategic Ploy Stratagem

In the midst of battle, Grey Knights can shut out pain, distraction and emotion to bring their psychic might to bear again and again.

Use this Stratagem in your Psychic phase. Select one **GREY KNIGHTS PSYKER** unit from your army. Until the end of the phase, that unit can attempt to manifest one more psychic power than normal.

FIGHT ON THE MOVE   1CP

Grey Knights – Strategic Ploy Stratagem

Personal teleporters grant exceptional manoeuvrability to those with the specialist skills to endure repeated and rapid submersions in the warp.

Use this Stratagem in your Movement phase, when a **GREY KNIGHTS TELEPORTER** unit from your army Falls Back. Until the end of the turn, that unit is still eligible to shoot and charge, even though it Fell Back.

HALOED IN SOULFIRE   1CP

Grey Knights – Strategic Ploy Stratagem

The blazing glare of ancient technology and the shrouding coils of the immaterium often linger, obscuring the Grey Knights presence.

Use this Stratagem in your Movement phase, when a **GREY KNIGHTS CORE** unit from your army is set up on the battlefield using the Teleport Strike ability. Until the start of your next turn, each time an attack is made against that unit, subtract 1 from that attack's hit roll.

UNTAINTED AND UNBOWED   2CP

Grey Knights – Strategic Ploy Stratagem

Utterly incorruptible, the warriors of the Order of Purifiers stand strong, even in the face of the darkest evils.

Use this Stratagem in any phase, when a **PURIFIER SQUAD** unit from your army is selected as the target of an attack. Until the end of the phase, each time an attack is allocated to a model in that unit, subtract 1 from the Damage characteristic of that attack (to a minimum of 1).

PSY-LANCE BOMBARDMENT   3CP

Grey Knights – Strategic Ploy Stratagem

When needs must, the Grey Knights can call down the awesome firepower of their orbital strike cruisers. A blinding column of energy lances down from the heavens, burning flesh to ash and reducing metal to heaps of molten slag.

Use this Stratagem in your Command phase, if a **GREY KNIGHTS WARLORD** from your army is on the battlefield. Select one point on the battlefield and place a marker on that point. At the start of your next Command phase, roll one D6 for each unit within 6" of the centre of that marker, adding 1 if the unit being rolled for is within 3" of the centre of the marker and subtracting 1 if the unit being rolled for is a **CHARACTER**. On a 2-5, that unit suffers D3 mortal wounds, and on a 6+, that unit suffers D6 mortal wounds. The marker is then removed. You can only use this Stratagem once.

THE NEED TO KNOW   1CP

Grey Knights – Strategic Ploy Stratagem

Adept in the precision removal of memories, the mind-wiping of informants and far more brutal means of information control, the Grey Knights maintain Humanity's ignorance of the Chapter.

You can only use this Stratagem if your army only contains **GREY KNIGHTS** Detachments. Use this Stratagem if you are playing a mission that requires you to select either secondary objectives or Agendas, after both players have revealed their selections. You can select one of your secondary objectives or Agendas, and replace it with a different one (make a note on your army roster as to your new selection and inform your opponent). All the normal rules for selecting secondary objectives and Agendas apply. If both players have a rule that allows them to select new secondary objectives or Agendas, both players make their new selections before revealing them simultaneously to their opponent.

ALLOY OF DISCIPLINES   1CP

Grey Knights – Strategic Ploy Stratagem

The noble elite of the Chapter, the Paladins are drawn from across the brotherhoods, bringing together a wealth of skill and powers.

Use this Stratagem in your Command phase. Select one **PALADIN** unit from your army. Select one psychic power from the Sanctic discipline that unit does not know to replace one of the psychic powers that it does.

MARTIAL PRESCIENCE   1CP

Grey Knights – Strategic Ploy Stratagem

With their superlative martial skills honed to perfection, Grey Knights can turn the enemy's blows against them.

Use this Stratagem in the Fight phase, when a **GREY KNIGHTS** unit that is Set to Defend is selected as the target of an attack made by an enemy model. Until the end of the phase, each time an unmodified save roll of 6 is made for a model in that unit, after the attacking model's unit has finished making its attacks, the attacking model's unit suffers 1 mortal wound.

STEELY ADVANCE   2CP

Grey Knights – Strategic Ploy Stratagem

With a coldly determined advance, the Grey Knights unleash a steady stream of devastating fire with unerring accuracy.

Use this Stratagem in your Movement phase, when a **Grey Knights Infantry** unit from your army makes a Normal Move. Until the end of the turn, that unit is considered to have Remained Stationary.

HEXAGRAMMIC WARDS   1CP

Grey Knights – Wargear Stratagem

Upon induction into the Chapter, every Grey Knight is trained to steel himself against psychic assaults.

Use this Stratagem in your opponent's Psychic phase, before a Deny the Witch test is taken for a **Grey Knights Psyker** unit from your army. When taking that test, roll one additional D6 and discard the lowest result.

TELEPORTATION SHUNT   2CP

Grey Knights – Wargear Stratagem

Like a cleansing fire, Grey Knights equipped with personal teleporters can sweep across the entire battlefield.

Use this Stratagem in your Movement phase, when a **Grey Knights Teleporter** unit from your army is selected to make a Normal Move. Instead of making a Normal Move with that unit, remove it from the battlefield and then set it back up on the battlefield, anywhere that is more than 9" away from any enemy models. A unit can only be selected for this Stratagem once per battle.

MISTS OF DEIMOS   1CP

Grey Knights – Wargear Stratagem

From hull-mounted launchers, Grey Knights' vehicles fire smoke grenades whose effects are boosted by the obscuring powers of their psychic crews and sometimes called the Mists of Deimos.

Use this Stratagem in your opponent's Shooting phase, when a **Grey Knights Smokescreen** unit from your army is selected as the target of an attack. Until the end of the phase, each time an attack is made against that unit, subtract 1 from that attack's hit roll.

TRUESILVER ARMOUR   2CP/3CP

Grey Knights – Wargear Stratagem

Grey Knights battle-plate incorporates litanies of purity, strands of sanctified silver and other sacred wards.

Use this Stratagem in any phase, when a **Grey Knights Core Infantry** unit from your army is selected as the target of an attack. Until the end of the phase, each time an attack is made against that unit, an unmodified wound roll of 1-3 for that attack fails, irrespective of any abilities that the weapon or the model making the attack may have. If that unit contains 5 or fewer models, this Stratagem costs 2CP; otherwise, it costs 3CP.

PSYBOLT AMMUNITION   1CP/2CP

Grey Knights – Wargear Stratagem

By entreating the machine spirit of his weapon with psychic incantations, a battle-brother can infuse the already deadly payload with explosive mental energy.

Use this Stratagem in your Shooting phase, when a **Grey Knights** unit from your army is selected to shoot. Until the end of the phase, each time a model in that unit makes a ranged attack with a bolt weapon (pg 104):

- An unmodified hit roll of 6 automatically wounds the target.
- Improve the Armour Penetration characteristic of that attack by 1.

If this unit has 6 or more models, this Stratagem costs 2CP; otherwise, it costs 1CP.

ZONE OF WARDING   1CP/2CP

Grey Knights – Wargear Stratagem

Nemesis warding staves contain multiple refractor field generators in their hafts. When primed with the wielder's psychic energy, they project a zone of force that repulses his enemies' attacks.

Use this Stratagem in any phase, when a **Grey Knights** unit from your army is selected as the target of a ranged attack. Until the end of the phase, while that unit contains a model equipped with a Nemesis warding stave, models in that unit have a 5+ invulnerable save (**Terminator** models instead have a 4+ invulnerable save). If that unit contains 5 or fewer models, this Stratagem costs 1CP; otherwise, it costs 2CP.

PSYK-OUT GRENADE   1CP

Grey Knights – Wargear Stratagem

Dabblers in unclean magics and xenos sorcerers suffer harrowing pain and confusion in the psi-shock caused by the particles released by these grenades.

Use this Stratagem in your Shooting phase, when a **Grey Knights Psyk-out Grenades** unit is selected to shoot. If that unit is not within Engagement Range of any enemy units, roll one D6: on a 2+, the closest enemy **Psyker** unit that is within 6" of and visible to your unit suffers Perils of the Warp.

FRAG ASSAULT LAUNCHERS   1CP

Grey Knights – Wargear Stratagem

These explosive charges shower the enemy in fiery shrapnel, forcing them to seek cover or suffer Titan's judgement.

Use this Stratagem at the start of your Charge phase. Select one **Grey Knights Assault Launchers** unit from your army and one enemy unit (excluding **Vehicle** or **Monster** units) within 9" of that unit. That enemy unit can either brace or duck for cover.

- If that unit braces, it suffers D3 mortal wounds.
- If that unit ducks for cover, then until the end of the turn, subtract 1 from the Attacks characteristic of models in that unit, and that unit cannot fire Overwatch or Set to Defend.

RELICS OF TITAN

If your army is led by a **Grey Knights Warlord**, you can, when mustering your army, give one of the following Relics of Titan to a **Grey Knights Character** model from your army. Named characters cannot be given any of the following Relics.

Note that some Relics replace one of the model's existing items of wargear. Where this is the case, you must, if you are using points values, still pay the cost of the wargear that is being replaced. Write down any Relics of Titan your models have on your army roster.

SOUL GLAIVE

Over centuries of war, a fraction of a Grey Knight's essence may imprint itself upon his weapon. In rare cases, this imprint is so strong that it persists after death, and another can wield the blade to combine their own psychic might with that of a fallen hero. The Soul Glaive is such a weapon, a halberd that was carried into battle by the 13th Supreme Grand Master of the Grey Knights, Lord Sylas Kalthorn, who defeated the Daemon Prince Ka'laedzar in single combat.

Model equipped with a Nemesis force halberd only. This Relic replaces a Nemesis force halberd and has the following profile:

WEAPON	RANGE	TYPE	S	AP	D
Soul Glaive	Melee	Melee	+2	-3	2

Abilities: Each time an attack is made with this weapon, you can re-roll the hit roll and you can re-roll the wound roll.

DESTROYER OF CRYS'YLLIX

This is the first Nemesis daemon hammer, upon which all others are based. It was forged by the legendary Reed Vanar, third Brother-Captain of the Exactors, and first used to shatter the Lord of Change known as Crys'yllix. Countless daemons have felt its wrath in the centuries since.

Model equipped with a Nemesis daemon hammer only. This Relic replaces a Nemesis daemon hammer and has the following profile:

WEAPON	RANGE	TYPE	S	AP	D
Destroyer of Crys'yllix	Melee	Melee	x2	-3	4

Abilities: Each time an attack is made with this weapon, subtract 1 from that attack's hit roll.

FURY OF DEIMOS

When the moon of Deimos was gifted to Titan by the Adeptus Mechanicus, it carried with it a ship loaded with some of the finest weapons the Imperium has ever created. Among them was the Fury of Deimos, a weapon crafted by the first Fabricator General of Mars in the aftermath of the Horus Heresy. Superior in accuracy, rate of fire and reliability to a lesser storm bolter, it is a relic whose secrets have long been forgotten.

Model equipped with a storm bolter or master-crafted storm bolter only. This Relic replaces a storm bolter or master-crafted storm bolter and has the following profile:

WEAPON	RANGE	TYPE	S	AP	D
Fury of Deimos	24"	Rapid Fire 3	5	-2	2

BANNER OF REFINING FLAME

This sacred banner records the most righteous purifications performed by strike forces and individual battle-brothers throughout the Grey Knights' history. The bearer can channel the resonance of this glorious past into their psychic attacks, blasting his foes to ash in a radiant burst of searing soulfire.

Ancient model only. The bearer can attempt to perform the following psychic action:

Refining Flame (Psychic Action – Warp Charge 6): In your Psychic phase, the bearer can attempt to perform this psychic action. If completed, each enemy unit within 6" of the bearer suffers D3 mortal wounds.

DOMINA LIBER DAEMONICA

This tome is said to be a relic of Supreme Grand Master Janus, he who mastered all six hundred and sixty-six words of banishment, each one painstakingly recorded on its pages. In times of need a hero of the Chapter will carry this book into battle, its bindings crackling with arcane energy as the words repel warp entities and send daemons howling back into the warp.

- Enemy **Daemon** units that are set up on the battlefield as Reinforcements cannot be set up within 12" of the bearer.
- The bearer has the following ability: '**Domina Liber Daemonica (Aura):** While an enemy **Daemon** unit is within 6" of this model, each time a Combat Attrition test is taken for that unit, subtract 1 from that test.'

CUIRASS OF SACRIFICE

This inner surface of this suit of armour is etched with the names of the many allies that fought and died alongside the Grey Knights in the eternal war against the daemonic. The Cuirass is a reminder to Titan's sons that such sacrifice must not be forgotten, and the wearer swears a solemn vow not to dishonour the names of those who have suffered such a fate whilst even an ounce of strength remains in his body.

Infantry model only.

- Add 1 to armour saving throws made for the bearer.
- Each time the bearer would lose a wound, roll one D6: on a 5+, that wound is not lost.

SANCTIC SHARD

An artefact recovered from the daemon-infested world of Gharelghast, this gleaming gem has been reconsecrated by several of the most senior members of the Chapter's Librarius. Binding the arcane object's auras with all six hundred and sixty-six words of cleansing, the Grey Knights succeeded in ridding the relic of any residual taint of Chaos whilst retaining its mysterious power.

Each time a Deny the Witch test is taken for the bearer, if the result of that test was an unmodified result of 8+ or it was greater than the result of the Psychic test, that Deny the Witch test is passed.

GYROTEMPORAL VAULT

Within this fist-sized artefact, a spindle of seemingly perpetual chrono-psychic energy is thought to spin like a miniature pulsar. What manner of ancient cabal or long-dead xenos tribe wrought it is unknown. Regardless, with the correctly applied incantations, temporal energy can be siphoned from its midnight-black surface and projected to alter the flow of time and the fortunes of war by empowering the bearer's allies with incredible speed.

The bearer can attempt to perform the following psychic action:

Gyrotemporal Empowerment (Psychic Action – Warp Charge 5): In your Psychic phase, the bearer can attempt to empower their allies. If this action is completed successfully, select one friendly **Grey Knights Core** or **Grey Knights Character** unit within 3" of the bearer. Until the start of your next Psychic phase, at the start of the Fight phase, if the selected unit is within Engagement Range of any enemy units, it can fight first that phase.

BLADE OF THE FORSWORN

Taken from the Chambers of Purity under only the direst of circumstances, the Blade of the Forsworn is a relic weapon whose origins are unknown to any outside the Purifier order. Whatever its history, the sword has proven its worth in many a battle against the Grey Knights' most hated adversaries.

Model equipped with a Nemesis force sword only. This Relic replaces a Nemesis force sword and has the following profile:

WEAPON	RANGE	TYPE	S	AP	D
Blade of the Forsworn	Melee	Melee	+1	-3	3

Abilities: Each time an attack is made with this weapon against a **Daemon** unit, an unmodified wound roll of 2+ successfully wounds the target. If that unit has the **Monster** or **Vehicle** keyword, an unmodified wound roll of 4+ successfully wounds the target instead.

SIGIL OF EXIGENCE

Forged by the Techmarine Dorvel urThann, this small chor-bronze icon contains a powerful personal teleport matrix and a trio of vigilant machine spirits. Their pre-cogitative psyroutines guard against attacks from afar, spiriting their host away from danger in a blaze of light.

Once per battle, in your opponent's Shooting phase, when the bearer is selected as the target of a ranged attacks it can activate this Relic. If it does, remove the bearer from the battlefield and then set it back up on the battlefield, anywhere that is more than 9" away from any enemy models. If the bearer is no longer an eligible target, your opponent can then select new eligible targets for any attacks that had targeted the bearer.

AUGURIUM SCROLLS

A gift from the Prognosticars of the Augurium, these scrolls contain predictions of the future, divined through the tireless work of legions of rigorously monitored Chapter serfs. Memorised by the Grey Knight, the empyric visions recorded upon the scrolls feed into the psychic matrices within his Nemesis weapon, and enable their bearer to form a kind of psychic muscle memory that makes him even deadlier in battle.

Model with a Nemesis weapon only. Each time the bearer is selected to fight, you can re-roll one hit roll and one wound roll when resolving the bearer's attacks.

STAVE OF SUPREMACY

This heavily warded Nemesis stave is engraved with runes that give it power over the energies of the warp across a wide area. The weapon was instrumental in the survival of the Grey Knights aboard the strike cruiser Titan's Hand when its Geller field collapsed in mid-warp transit.

Model equipped with a Nemesis warding stave only. The bearer has the following ability: '**Stave of Supremacy (Aura):** While an enemy unit is within 18" of this model, each time a Psychic test is taken for that unit, it suffers Perils of the Warp on any roll of a double.'

KANTU VAMBRACE

This curved layer of silvered ceramite was recovered from the pyrrhic victory upon the death world of Kantu. The selfless defence of Kantu by the Grey Knights has coalesced into this vambrace, instilling the bearer with a sense of immovable resolve. With the spirits of such lost brothers strengthening his will, he withstands the most terrible of mystical onslaughts and shrugs off esoteric attacks.

Infantry model only.

- Each time the bearer would lose a wound as a result of a mortal wound, roll one D6: on a 4+, that wound is not lost.
- Each time an attack is allocated to the bearer, subtract 1 from the Damage characteristic of that attack (to a minimum of 1).

ARTISAN NULLIFIER MATRIX

A remnant from the Grey Knights' earliest days, this advanced psychic hood utilises powerful psy-tech long since lost to the adepts of the Chapter, offering its wearer even greater protection from the soul-hunting predators of the warp.

Librarian model only. The bearer gains the following ability: '**Artisan Nullifier Matrix (Aura):** While a friendly **Grey Knights Psyker** unit is within 9" of this model, each time a Psychic test is taken for that unit, it does not suffer Perils of the Warp.'

AETHERIC CONDUIT

This ancient device, thought to date from the Dark Age of Technology, allows the bearer to channel their psychic energies through its complex network of components to directly manipulate the most delicate of damaged vehicle systems.

Techmarine model only. Each time the bearer repairs a model using its Blessing of the Omnissiah ability, that model regains up to 3 lost wounds instead of up to D3.

DOMINUS DISCIPLINE

Before the battle, generate the psychic powers for **PSYKER** models from your army that know powers from the Dominus discipline using the table below. You can either roll one D6 to generate each power randomly (re-rolling duplicate results), or you can select which powers the **PSYKER** knows.

'The daemon has many forms. You must know them all. You must tell the daemon from his disguise and root him out from the hidden places.

Trust no one. Trust not even yourself. It is better to die in vain than to live in abomination. The zealous martyr is praised for his valour, the craven and the unready are justly abhorred.'

- *Excerpt from* The First Book of Indoctrinations

1. GATE OF INFINITY
The psyker punches a corridor through the roiling immaterium, allowing him to cross great distances in the blink of an eye.

Blessing: *Gate of Infinity* has a warp charge value of 7. If manifested, select one friendly **GREY KNIGHTS PSYKER** unit within 18" of this **PSYKER**. Remove that unit from the battlefield and then set it back up on the battlefield, anywhere that is more than 9" away from any enemy models.

2. EMPYRIC AMPLIFICATION
In ritualistic patterns, the psyker overlays a complex web of blessed, psychic amplification around the doomed foe. Matching the intricate martial methods of his brother knights, each strike with their psychically empowered weapons through this field drives more of their manifested power into the enemy.

Malediction: *Empyric Amplification* has a warp charge value of 7. If manifested, select one enemy unit within 12" of and visible to this **PSYKER**. Until the start of your next Psychic phase, each time an attack made with a Nemesis or psi weapon (pg 104) is allocated to a model in that unit, add 1 to the Damage characteristic of that attack.

3. SANCTUARY
Chanting words of warding, the psyker creates a zone of light around him that can both protect him from harm and repel daemonic creatures.

Blessing: *Sanctuary* has a warp charge value of 6. If manifested, select one friendly **GREY KNIGHTS** unit within 18" of this **PSYKER**. Until the start of your next Psychic phase, models in that unit have a 4+ invulnerable save.

4. VORTEX OF DOOM
The psyker tears a rift between realspace and the warp, condemning his foes to total oblivion.

Witchfire: *Vortex of Doom* has a warp charge value of 7. If manifested, select the closest enemy unit within 12" of and visible to this **PSYKER**: each other enemy unit within 3" of the selected unit suffers 1 mortal wound, and then the selected unit suffers 2D3 mortal wounds. If the model manifesting this power has the Psychic Epitome Warlord Trait, only the unit you selected suffers the additional mortal wound from that trait, not those other enemy units within 3" of it.

5. WARP SHAPING
The psyker draws deep from the very fabric of the warp, moulding it to serve his will and the needs of his battle-brothers.

Blessing: *Warp Shaping* has a warp charge value of 4. If manifested, select one Tide of the Warp (pg 81) that has not been dominant for your army during this battle. Your army's currently dominant Tide of the Warp is changed to the selected Tide of the Warp.

6. GHOSTLY BONDS
Subtly manipulating the invisible barrier separating the immaterium from the material realm, the psyker causes imperfect wrinkles and bulges within its fabric to gather around his opponents, pushing back against their advance and dragging at their momentum like a spiritual halter.

Malediction: *Ghostly Bonds* has a warp charge value of 5. If manifested, select one enemy unit within 18" of and visible to this **PSYKER**. Until the start of your next Psychic phase, halve that unit's Move characteristic.

SANCTIC DISCIPLINE

A unit's datasheet will specify which, if any, psychic powers it knows from the Sanctic discipline. If a unit's datasheet states that it can know any psychic power from this discipline, then, before the battle, you can either roll one D6 to generate that power randomly, or you can select which power that **PSYKER** knows.

Psychic Confluence

Each time a **GREY KNIGHTS PSYKER** is selected to manifest psychic powers, it can attempt to manifest any of the psychic powers that it knows from the Sanctic discipline even if that power has already been attempted to be manifested by another unit that phase. Each time such a unit attempts to manifest such a power, then until the end of the phase, add 1 to that power's warp charge value for each other attempt that has been made to manifest it by a unit from your army that phase, whether the attempt was successful or not.

1. ASTRAL AIM

The psyker reaches out to the minds of his fellow battle-brothers, mystically guiding their aim to the chosen target.

Blessing: *Astral Aim* has a warp charge value of 6. If manifested, until the start of your next Psychic phase:

- Each time this **PSYKER**'s unit is selected to shoot, you can re-roll one hit roll when resolving that unit's attacks.
- Each time a model in this **PSYKER**'s unit makes a ranged attack, the target does not receive the benefits of cover against that attack.

2. PURGE SOUL

The psyker draws upon every ounce of willpower he possesses to purge the evil from his foes' souls, scouring every trace of corruption.

Witchfire: *Purge Soul* has a warp charge value of 6. If manifested, select one enemy unit within 12" of and visible to this **PSYKER** that has not already been selected for this power this phase. Then, roll one D6 and add this **PSYKER**'s Leadership characteristic to the result. Your opponent then rolls one D6 and adds that unit's Leadership characteristic to the result.

- If your total is higher than your opponent's, the selected unit suffers D3 mortal wounds.
- If your total is equal to your opponent's, the selected unit suffers 1 mortal wound.
- If your total is less than your opponent's, nothing happens.

3. HAMMERHAND

Focusing the raging power of his mind, the psyker augments the strength of his comrades to the point where they can crush flesh and bone with a single blow.

Blessing: *Hammerhand* has a warp charge value of 5. If manifested, until the start of your next Psychic phase, each time a model in this **PSYKER**'s unit makes a melee attack, you can re-roll the wound roll.

4. PURIFYING FLAME

The pellucid fire of the psyker's soul is released in a wave of empyric flame, burning the essences of the unworthy.

Witchfire: *Purifying Flame* has a warp charge value of 5. If manifested, the closest enemy unit within 9" of and visible to this **PSYKER** suffers 3 mortal wounds. If the result of the Psychic test was 11+, that unit suffers D3+3 mortal wounds instead.

5. ARMOURED RESILIENCE

The psyker channels the primordial energies of the empyrean through himself, infusing the armour of his allies with its power, hardening the ceramite beyond what could be achieved by Human artifice.

Blessing: *Armoured Resilience* has a warp charge value of 6. If manifested, until the start of your next Psychic phase, add 1 to armour saving throws made for models in this **PSYKER**'s unit.

6. ETHEREAL CASTIGATION

Hardening his soul, the psyker directs his brothers' lethal fire before spiriting them away so quickly that any witnessing the ruin of their weapons' blessed verdict would swear it came from thin air.

Blessing: *Ethereal Castigation* has a warp charge value of 6. If manifested, this **PSYKER**'s unit can shoot as if were your Shooting phase, and then it can make a Normal Move as if it were your Movement phase. After making this move and/or resolving these shooting attacks, until the end of the turn, this **PSYKER**'s unit cannot make a Normal Move, Advance, charge, or shoot.

'We will split the warp stuff of their flesh, we will incinerate their sickening visages, smite down those who dare raise a blade against us and crush underfoot those who slink away. We will enshrine this victory alongside the Purgation of Archaenologos. These soulless creatures will learn to fear the Swordbearers not just this day, but for the eternity of their pained and anguished existence!'

- Terminator Justicar Apollon Cestaerin, 1st Brotherhood

LITANIES OF PURITY

All **Grey Knights Priests** know the *Litany of Expulsion* (see below). In addition, before the battle, generate the additional litanies for **Priest** models from your army that know litanies from the Litanies of Purity using the table below. You can either roll one D6 to generate each litany randomly (re-rolling duplicate results), or you can select which litanies the **Priest** knows.

LITANY OF EXPULSION (AURA)
Intoning the unholy crimes of the Grey Knights' enemies, the Chaplain fills his battle-brothers with an efficacy of purpose as they slay their foes.

If this litany is inspiring, then while a friendly **Grey Knights Core** or **Grey Knights Character** unit is within 6" of this **Priest**, each time a model in that unit makes a melee attack, you can re-roll the hit roll.

1. WORDS OF POWER
The Chaplain clears his mind, focusing all of his willpower into fuelling the force weapons of his brother warriors.

If this litany is inspiring, select one friendly **Grey Knights Core** or **Grey Knights Character** unit within 6" of this **Priest**. Each time a model in that unit makes a melee attack with a Nemesis weapon (pg 104), an unmodified wound roll of 6 successfully wounds the target one additional time and, if the Tide of Convergence is dominant for your army, the target also suffers 1 mortal wound.

2. INTONEMENT FOR GUIDANCE
The Chaplain leads his brothers in a ritual of centring, allowing the Grey Knights to better exploit their warp-sight talents.

If this litany is inspiring, select one friendly **Grey Knights Core** or **Grey Knights Character** unit within 6" of this **Priest**. Each time a model in that unit makes a ranged attack, you can ignore any or all hit roll and Ballistic Skill modifiers.

3. PSALM OF PURITY (AURA)
The Chaplain exhorts his charges to purify the realms of the Emperor with the cleansing fire of their weapons.

If this litany is inspiring, while a friendly **Grey Knights Core** or **Grey Knights Character** unit is within 6" of this **Priest**, each time a model in that unit makes a ranged attack, on an unmodified wound roll of 6, improve the Armour Penetration characteristic of that attack by 1.

4. REFRAIN OF CONVERGENCE
The Chaplain recites the Grey Knights' words of sanctity, his voice rising to a crescendo as he fights to cast down the malign sorcery of the enemy.

If this litany is inspiring, select one unit within 6" of this **Priest**:

- That unit, and the models it contains, stop being affected by any psychic powers that had been affecting it that had been manifested by an enemy unit.
- Until the start of your next Command phase, that unit, and the models it contains, are not affected by any psychic powers manifested by enemy units.

5. RECITATION OF PROJECTION
The Chaplain guides his brothers in sacred rituals, the shared commune of their psychic brotherhood amplifying the kinetic and psychic energies of their weapons to hammer their foes from afar.

If this litany is inspiring, select one friendly **Grey Knights Core** or **Grey Knights Character** unit within 6" of this **Priest**. Until the start of your next Command phase, add 6" to the Range characteristic of bolt and psi weapons (pg 104) models in that unit are equipped with; if the Tide of Convergence (pg 81) is dominant for your army, then add 6" to the Range of bolt weapons but only add 3" to the Range of psi weapons that models in the unit are equipped with (note that with the similar bonus conferred by the Tide of Convergence, this means that the total Range increase of Psi weapons will be then be 9").

6. INVOCATION OF FOCUS (AURA)
The Chaplain's words sharpen the minds of the Grey Knights who hear him, honing their psychic affinities upon brotherhood and duty in the face of inhuman malignancy.

If this litany is inspiring, while a friendly **Grey Knights Core** or **Grey Knights Character** unit is within 6" of this **Priest**, each time that unit attempts to manifest a Blessing psychic power, add 1 to that attempt's Psychic test.

WARLORD TRAITS

If a **GREY KNIGHTS CHARACTER** model is your **WARLORD**, you can use the Grey Knights Warlord Traits table below to determine what Warlord Trait they have. You can either roll one D6 to randomly generate one, or you can select one.

1. DAEMON-SLAYER

The warlord is a master of the rituals of banishing and unbinding, able to sever his daemonic foes' connection to the warp and crush their mortal forms.

- Each time this **WARLORD** fights, if it made a charge move this turn, then until that fight is resolved, add 1 to its Attacks characteristic.
- Each time this **WARLORD** makes a melee attack against a **DAEMON** unit, invulnerable saving throws cannot be made against that attack.

2. HAMMER OF RIGHTEOUSNESS

Fortified by the unflagging will of his battle-brothers, the warlord lays into the foe like the hammer of the Emperor.

Each time this **WARLORD** makes a melee attack, if it made a charge move, was charged or performed a Heroic Intervention this turn, add 1 to that attack's wound roll.

3. UNYIELDING ANVIL (AURA)

The inspiring presence of the warlord reminds the Grey Knights that there can be no retreat, no matter the odds arrayed against them.

While a friendly **GREY KNIGHTS CORE** or **GREY KNIGHTS CHARACTER** unit is within 6" of this **WARLORD**, that unit has the Objective Secured ability (see the Warhammer 40,000 Core Book). If a model in such a unit already has this ability, that model counts as one additional model when determining control of an objective marker.

4. FIRST TO THE FRAY

The warlord is an eager, hot-blooded warrior, ever the first to leap into the fray. Inspired by such zealous bravery, his battle-brothers are never far behind.

- Add 1 to Advance and charge rolls made for this **WARLORD**.
- If this **WARLORD** has made a charge move this turn, then until the end of the turn, each time a friendly **GREY KNIGHTS CORE** unit declares a charge against an enemy unit that is within Engagement Range of this **WARLORD**, add 1 to the charge roll made for that unit.

5. NEMESIS LORD

Over the course of countless battles the warlord has mastered the art of single combat. He is a force of destruction upon the battlefield, wielding his Nemesis weapon with preternatural skill.

Each time this **WARLORD** makes a melee attack with a Nemesis weapon (pg 104), an unmodified hit roll of 6 automatically wounds the target.

6. PSYCHIC EPITOME

The warlord employs his immense psychic potential as a conduit for his battle-brothers' empyric powers, channelling greater energy into their sorcerous strikes.

At the start of each of your Psychic phases, select one friendly **GREY KNIGHTS PSYKER** unit within 6" of this **WARLORD**. Until the end of the phase, each time that unit manifests a Witchfire psychic power, when resolving that psychic power, if an enemy unit suffers any mortal wounds, that enemy unit suffers 1 additional mortal wound.

NAMED CHARACTERS AND WARLORD TRAITS

If one of the following characters gains a Warlord Trait, they must have the one shown below:

Named Character	Warlord Trait
Lord Kaldor Draigo	Daemon-slayer
Grand Master Voldus	Loremaster (pg 48)
Brother-Captain Stern	Unyielding Anvil
Castellan Crowe	Hammer of Righteousness

CHAPTER APPROVED RULES

If every model in your army (excluding **AGENTS OF THE IMPERIUM** and **UNALIGNED** units) has the **GREY KNIGHTS** keyword, and your **WARLORD** has the **GREY KNIGHTS** keyword, you can, if you are playing a matched play battle that instructs you to select secondary objectives (e.g. a mission from the Eternal War mission pack in the Warhammer 40,000 Core Book) select one of them to be from the **GREY KNIGHTS** secondary objectives listed below.

Like all other secondary objectives, each of the secondary objectives listed below has a category, and they follow all the normal rules for secondary objectives (for example, when you select secondary objectives, you cannot choose more than one from each category, you can score no more than 15 victory points from each secondary objective you select during the mission etc.).

PURGE THE ENEMY

DESTROY THE DAEMON

End Game Objective

The Grey Knights were created for a sacred and singular duty: the destruction of the daemonic in all its forms. From the insidious to the monstrous, all must fall before the Sons of Titan.

If you select this objective, you score victory points for each unit that was destroyed in the battle by a **GREY KNIGHTS** unit from your army as follows:

- **DAEMON PRIMARCH** unit– score 5 victory points
- Any other **DAEMON MONSTER** unit– score 3 victory points
- **DAEMON VEHICLE** unit– score 3 victory points
- Any other **DAEMON** unit – score 1 victory point

NO MERCY, NO RESPITE

TELEPORT ASSAULT

Progressive Objective

The Grey Knights' empyric defences ward them against the chill touch of the warp. Emerging from the actinic glare of teleportation, they crush their foes in a sudden hammerblow of fury before the enemy has any chance to strike back.

Score 3 victory points at the end of the battle round if one or more enemy units were destroyed by a **GREY KNIGHTS** model from your army that was set up on the battlefield using the Teleport Strike ability, the Teleportation Shunt Stratagem or the Gate of Infinity psychic power during that battle round.

WARPCRAFT

PURIFYING RITUAL

Progressive Objective

The corruption seething over this vital area cannot be allowed to weaken the barriers holding back the warp. It must be ritually purified, one psychic node at a time. So it has been foreseen.

Score a number of victory points at the end of the battle round as shown in the table below, with the number of victory points scored depending on how many units from your army successfully completed the following psychic action that battle round:

Purifying Ritual (Psychic Action – Warp Charge 5): In your Psychic phase, this action can be performed by any number of units in your army. In your Psychic phase, if a **GREY KNIGHTS PSYKER** unit from your army is within 3" of an objective marker, it can attempt to purify it by performing this psychic action. Each objective marker cannot be purified more than once in the same turn.

PURIFYING RITUAL	
NUMBER OF PURIFIED OBJECTIVES	**VICTORY POINTS SCORED**
1	1
2	2
3	4
4+	6

NAME GENERATOR

If you wish to generate a name for your heroic Grey Knights, you can roll a D66 and consult the tables or simply pick any combination that feels appropriate. To roll a D66, simply roll two D6, one after the other — the first represents tens and the second represents digits, giving you a result between 11 and 66.

D66	FORENAME	D66	SURNAME
11	Alaric	11	Geronitan
12	Anval	12	Vortimer
13	Ahakim	13	Ignatius
14	Dokelus	14	Issad
15	Blaris	15	Edeon
16	Icanus	16	Neodan
21	Martesias	21	Phoros
22	Galan	22	Zaebus
23	Retius	23	Thawn
24	Jarius	24	Nedth
25	Cyntanus	25	Gruila
26	Pellastis	26	Tekios
31	Axatinos	31	Thamare
32	Garran	32	Alegssus
33	Vitennias	33	Esdrios
34	Xeridon	34	Thule
35	Jakaton	35	Simedes
36	Jaric	36	Arelis
41	Caddon	41	Ortyrian
42	Aldrios	42	Akantar
43	Beliaros	43	Cordacus
44	Kardoch	44	Massius
45	Astokar	45	Vibova
46	Galarr	46	Tydes
51	Xerikim	51	Elgon
52	Archaddeus	52	Cybaddas
53	Medemeion	53	Adantor
54	Cortane	54	Sorak
55	Janutrius	55	Invio
56	Furoza	56	Kai
61	Drystan	61	Solor
62	Ortus	62	Varn
63	Lushian	63	Trevan
64	Elrin	64	Morretus
65	Arion	65	Cybasi
66	Valdar	66	Santor

CRUSADE RULES

In this section you'll find additional rules for playing Crusade battles with Grey Knights, such as additional Agendas, Battle Traits and Crusade Relics that are bespoke to Grey Knights units. You can find out more about Crusade armies in the Warhammer 40,000 Core Book.

This section contains the following additional rules:

AGENDAS

Grey Knights units attempt to achieve unique Agendas in Crusade battles, which can be found on page 71. These Agendas represent the unique goals of Grey Knights armies on the battlefield and help to reflect their particular methods of waging war. You can find out more about Agendas in the Crusade mission packs, such as that presented in the Warhammer 40,000 Core Book.

REQUISITIONS

Grey Knights armies have access to a number of unique Requisitions, suited to their methods for waging war. You can find these on page 72.

HONOURED TITLES

Honoured Titles are the roles and responsibilities held by the Grand Masters of the brotherhoods, and can be found on page 73. Each confers a new ability on that Grand Master and allows you to better represent your selected brotherhood on the battlefield.

CRUSADE RELICS

In addition to the Crusade Relics presented in the Warhammer 40,000 Core Book, Grey Knights characters can quest to search for one of the Crusade relics described on page 74; these Relics are unique to the Grey Knights, and are mighty symbols of martial prowess for any hero of worth from that mysterious Chapter.

BATTLE TRAITS

Grey Knights units can select one of the Battle Traits presented on page 75 as they gain experience and are promoted in your Crusade force. These help to better reflect the unique upgrades and Battle Honours that are bestowed to Grey Knights units.

PSYCHIC FORTITUDES

Powerful psykers all, the Grey Knights can choose to hone their psychic might with a new selection of Psychic Fortitudes when they gain a Battle Honour. You can find these on page 76.

DAEMONIC NEMESIS

Some Grey Knights will encounter the same daemonic entities several times over their lifetimes. Some of these entities are known to delight in tormenting these warriors, leading them a merry dance across the galaxy, evading their divine retribution. For others, their hubris leads to their downfall as they are tracked down and banished. You can find the rules for creating and battling your daemonic nemesis on page 77.

The deployment of Terminators to combat a sorcerous cult on Bephreba proves the wisdom in the Prognosticars' vision of high treachery when the blasphemous Word Bearers reveal themselves as the true architects of a vast ritual.

AGENDAS

If your Crusade army includes any **Grey Knights** units, you can select one Agenda from the Grey Knights Agendas, listed below. This is a new category of Agendas, and follows all the normal rules for Agendas (for example, when you select Agendas, you cannot choose more than one from each category).

NO WITNESSES

Grey Knights Agenda

The unholy deeds at play here leave no option but to ensure the eradication of all those without the highest dispensation.

At the end of the battle, if there are no models from your opponent's army on the battlefield, and there are no models other than **Grey Knights** and **Ordo Malleus** units remaining on the battlefield, each **Grey Knights** unit from your army that is on the battlefield gains 3 experience points.

PSYCHIC FELLOWSHIP

Grey Knights Agenda

The Grey Knights forge psychic bonds of brotherhood and sacred rites with their fellow daemonhunters.

Keep a Psychic Fellowship tally for each **Grey Knights Psyker** unit from your army. Each time a unit successfully completes the Psychic Fellowship psychic action (see below), add 1 to that unit's Psychic Fellowship tally. If you selected this Agenda, then **Grey Knights Psyker** units in your army can attempt the following psychic action:

Psychic Fellowship (Psychic Action - Warp Charge 4): One **Grey Knights Psyker** unit from your army can attempt to perform this psychic action in your Psychic phase if it is within 6" of two other friendly **Grey Knights Psyker** units.

Each unit gains 1 experience point for each mark on their Psychic Fellowship tally.

THE ANCIENT ENEMY

Grey Knights Agenda

It is by his tally of sundered and banished warp spawn that a warrior of the 666th Chapter is often known to his brothers, if not to the Imperium.

Keep an Ancient Enemy tally for each **Grey Knights** unit in your army. At the end of each phase, if a **Grey Knights** unit from your army has destroyed any of the following units, add the listed number of marks to that unit's tally:

- **Daemon Primarch** – 6 marks
- **Nemesis** (see page 77) – 4 marks
- Any other **Daemon Monster** unit– 2 marks
- **Daemon Vehicle** unit – 2 marks
- Any other **Daemon** unit – 1 mark

Each unit gains 1 experience point for every 2 marks on its Ancient Enemy tally.

UNCOVER PROPHECY

Grey Knights Agenda

Visions have hinted at an apocalyptic evil surrounding the enemy's influential leaders. Their futures must be excised from existence with absolute surety.

Keep a Prophecy tally for each **Grey Knights** unit in your army. Add 1 to a unit's Prophecy tally each time it destroys an enemy **Character** unit with a melee attack.

Each unit gains a number of experience points equal to their Prophecy tally.

CLEANSE GROUND

Grey Knights Agenda

Preordained sites of empyric power must be psychically cleansed of corruption, lest the warp use them as a means of ingress.

Keep a Cleanse Ground tally for each **Grey Knights Psyker** unit from your army. Each time a unit successfully completes the Cleanse Ground psychic action, add 1 to that unit's Cleanse Ground tally.

If you selected this Agenda, then **Grey Knights Psyker** units in your army can attempt the following psychic action:

Cleanse Ground (Psychic Action - Warp Charge 4): One **Grey Knights Psyker** unit from your army can attempt to perform this psychic action in your Psychic phase if it is within range of an objective marker that has not already had this psychic action performed on it.

Each unit gains 2 experience points if their Cleanse Ground tally is at least 1.

BANISHMENT

Grey Knights Agenda

Your nemesis is here! Send them back to the warp before they can enact their nefarious plans.

You can only select this Agenda if the **Nemesis** unit is part of your opponent's army. If the **Nemesis Hunter** unit destroys the **Nemesis** unit, the **Nemesis Hunter** unit gains 5 experience points.

We burned the forge world of Hjorgan Ultima for the imprudent sins of one priest's avarice. A serf population of over four billion, manufactora whose tithes supported three war zones, some thousands of adherents to the Cult Mechanicus and a reputed sub-pattern STC. Yet by our hand were twelve more systems spared such horror.

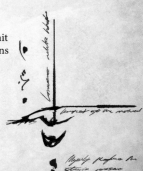

THE LIBER DAEMONICA

Every Grey Knight carries a copy of the Liber Daemonica in a ceramite case on his breastplate. These gnarled tomes contain the Chapter's rites of battle, the prayers of sanctity and details of the traditional duties every Grey Knight must fulfil, from recruit to Supreme Grand Master.

The Liber Daemonica is an enduring symbol of the Grey Knight's devotion to his mission, and contains the cardinal tenets of lore culled from the dark knowledge caged within the Sanctum Sanctorum's walls. The books themselves are also potent talismans in their own right, with pages illuminated in silver and bound to a spine carved from the thigh bone of a martyred saint. Placed over the Grey Knights' genetically engineered hearts, the tome resonates with the warrior's own purity and helps shield his spirit from malevolent influence.

Though most end their service to the Chapter with the warrior's own, interred alongside him in the Dead Fields, some copies – imprinted with a portion of his indomitable spirit – are encased in individual shrines within the Hall of Champions. As much an armament against the daemonic as any blade, these are proudly placed alongside the Chapter's greatest weapons.

REQUISITIONS

If your Crusade force includes any **GREY KNIGHTS** units, you can spend Requisition points (RPs) on any of the following Requisitions in addition to those presented in the Warhammer 40,000 Core Book.

A PURITY BEYOND DEATH   1RP

A mortally wounded Grey Knight may be interred in the sarcophagus of a Dreadnought, allowing him to continue destroying his daemonic foes in a new, even mightier, form.

Purchase this Requisition when a **GREY KNIGHTS CHARACTER** unit (excluding **VEHICLE** units) from your Crusade force gains their second or subsequent Battle Scar. Remove that unit from your Order of Battle and replace it with a **GREY KNIGHTS DREADNOUGHT** unit. You cannot purchase this Requisition if doing so would cause your total Power Level to exceed your Crusade force's Supply Limit. The new Dreadnought starts with the same number of experience points as the unit it replaced and gains the appropriate number of Battle Honours for its rank. If the unit that was replaced was a **NEMESIS HUNTER**, the new unit gains this keyword.

BATTLE THE MIGHTIEST FOES   1RP

A Grand Master can call upon any and all of the equipment available to his Brotherhood in his lifelong battle against the daemonic. This includes the option to go to war piloting a mighty Nemesis Dreadknight.

Purchase this Requisition at any time. Select one **GREY KNIGHTS GRAND MASTER** unit. Remove that unit from your Order of Battle and replace it with a **GRAND MASTER NEMESIS DREADKNIGHT** unit. You cannot purchase this Requisition if doing so would cause your total Power Level to exceed your Crusade force's Supply Limit. The new unit starts with the same number of experience points as the unit it replaced and gains the appropriate number of Battle Honours for its rank. If the unit that was replaced was a **NEMESIS HUNTER**, the new unit gains this keyword.

CONSULT THE PROGNOSTICARS   1RP

The Prognosticars provide crucial information about events that will unfold during the battle.

Purchase this Requisition at any time. Select one **GREY KNIGHTS CHARACTER** model from your Crusade force that does not have a Vision of the Augurium or a Gift of the Prescient (pg 54-56). Select either Visions of the Augurium or Gifts of the Prescient, and roll one D6; that model gains the Vision or Gift that corresponds to the result (if a result is rolled that another model in your Crusade force already has, roll again). Make a note on the unit's Crusade card of the result, but do not increase that unit's Power Rating or Crusade points. Once the Vision or Gift has been used, it is removed from that unit's Crusade card.

DEEDS OF LEGEND   1RP

It is the tragedy of the Grey Knights that their greatest successes will never be known to any outside their own Chapter. Those few who have seen or heard the deeds of the mightiest of their heroes hold these warriors in high esteem.

Purchase this Requisition at any time. Select one **GREY KNIGHTS CHARACTER** unit from your Order of Battle with 71 or more experience points. The selected unit gains one additional Battle Honour (this does not count towards the maximum number of Battle Honours a unit can have). Each unit can only be selected for this Requisition once.

HONOURED TITLES

Honoured Titles are a new type of Battle Honour that can be given to **GREY KNIGHTS GRAND MASTER** units. When a **GREY KNIGHTS GRAND MASTER** unit from your army would gain a Battle Honour, you can instead choose for it to gain one of the Honoured Titles listed below. Each **GRAND MASTER** can only have a single Honoured Title, and your Order of Battle cannot include more than one **GRAND MASTER** from the same **<BROTHERHOOD>** with the same Honoured Title. As with any Battle Honour, make a note on the unit's Crusade card when it gains an Honoured Title, and increase its Crusade points total by 1.

STEWARD OF THE ARMOURY

Traditionally held by the Grand Master of the 1st Brotherhood, this title signifies its bearer's duties associated with the Chapter's armoured vehicles and materiel maintained by the Techmarines, as well as the swift distribution of such equipment to strike forces active throughout the galaxy.

SWORDBEARERS GRAND MASTER only. If this Grand Master is part of your Crusade force, then the Rearm and Resupply Requisition costs 0 Requisition points if the unit being Rearmed and Resupplied is a **GREY KNIGHTS** unit.

ADMIRAL OF THE FLEET

With the responsibility to ensure the ready deployment and effective use of the Chapter's large number of warships, the Grand Master of the 2nd Brotherhood develops an instinctive feel for their precision capabilities.

BLADES OF VICTORY GRAND MASTER only.

- If this Grand Master is on the battlefield, you can use the Psy-lance Bombardment Stratagem (pg 60) twice during the battle instead of once.
- If this Grand Master is on the battlefield, each time you use the Psy-lance Bombardment Stratagem, it costs 1 Command point instead of 3.

WARDEN OF THE LIBRARIUS

This title has been held by the Grand Master of the 3rd Brotherhood for tens of millennia. In this role he oversees the duties of the Chapter's Librarians, ensuring the Grey Knights have access to their accumulated wisdom in their time of need.

WARDMAKERS GRAND MASTER only. If this Grand Master is part of your Crusade force, then the Psychic Meditations Requisition costs 0 Requisition points if the unit selected is a **GREY KNIGHTS PSYKER** unit.

KEEPER OF THE AUGURIUM

The Grand Master of the 4th Brotherhood preserves the Chapter's Prognosticars, safeguarding their rituals and meditations. Through his duties connected with their silver citadel, he has access to the gathered foresight of the Chapter and is highly adept at using it to his advantage in battle.

PRESCIENT BRETHREN GRAND MASTER only. If this Grand Master is part of your Crusade army and you are the Attacker, then you start the battle with an additional 2 Command points.

PROTECTOR OF THE SANCTUM SANCTORUM

The Sanctum Sanctorum is the repository of the Chapter's collected history and their knowledge of the daemonic. The Grand Master of the 5th Brotherhood ensures its security, for all manner of powerful artefacts and arcane relics line its vaults.

PRESERVERS GRAND MASTER only. If this Grand Master is part of your Crusade force, then the Relic Requisition costs 0 Requisition points if the model gaining the Relic is a **GREY KNIGHTS** unit.

HIGH SENESCHAL OF THE FORTRESS

Managing the complex assignment of elements stationed on Titan to fresh strike forces - while maintaining the home world's sanctity - the 6th Brotherhood's Grand Master is a master defensive strategist.

RAPIERS GRAND MASTER only. If this Grand Master is part of your Crusade army and you are the Defender, then you start the battle with an additional 2 Command points.

REPRESENTATIVE TO THE INQUISITION

The Grand Master of the 7th Brotherhood works closely with the Inquisition, and in so doing maintains the layers of absolute secrecy around the Chapter.

EXACTORS GRAND MASTER only.

- If this Grand Master is part of your Crusade army, then when you select Agendas for that battle, you can select one additional Agenda and when all Agendas have been revealed, discard one of your Agendas.
- If this Grand Master is part of your Crusade force, and it also includes any **INQUISITOR** units, all **EXACTORS** units on the battlefield are treated as being within range of the Unquestionable Wisdom ability while there are any **INQUISITOR** units on the battlefield.

KNIGHT COMMANDER OF THE RECRUITS

The recruitment and training of new brothers of the Chapter is the responsibility of the Grand Master of the 8th Brotherhood, maintaining the exacting standards expected of the warriors of the 666th Chapter.

SILVER BLADES GRAND MASTER only. If this Grand Master is part of your Crusade force, then the Fresh Recruits Requisition costs 0 Requisition points if the unit gaining the Fresh Recruits is a **GREY KNIGHTS** unit.

> If **GRAND MASTER VOLDUS** is included in your Crusade force, he automatically gains the Warden of the Librarius Honoured Title, even though he cannot normally gain any Battle Honours.

CRUSADE RELICS

When a GREY KNIGHTS CHARACTER model gains a Crusade Relic, you can instead select one of the Relics listed below. All the usual rules for selecting Crusade Relics, as described in the Warhammer 40,000 Core Book, apply.

ARTIFICER RELICS

Bones of Falkothan

A former Grand Master of the 3rd Brotherhood, Falkothan was a ferociously potent psyker. His bones - encased within a sanctified silver reliquary whenever taken from the Dead Fields - retain a portion of his psychic might.

Once per battle, at the start of any battle round, the bearer can draw upon the power of the bones. If they do so, then until the end of that battle round, the bearer has a 3+ invulnerable save.

Armour of Caladys

Every inch of this armour was inscribed with hexagrammic wards over the course of Grand Master Caladys' long lifetime. In the presence of the daemonic, these engravings glow bright, blinding nearby malevolent entities with divine power.

Each time a DAEMON unit makes a melee attack against the bearer, subtract 1 from that attack's hit roll.

ANTIQUITY RELICS

A GREY KNIGHTS CHARACTER model of Heroic rank or higher can be given one of the following Antiquity Relics instead of one of the ones presented in the Warhammer 40,000 Core Book. Add 1 to a unit's total Crusade points for each Antiquity Relic it has – this is in addition to the +1 from gaining a Battle Honour, for a total of +2.

Nullbolts

These rare shells blast shards of warp-dampening material into the victim, severing their connection to the immaterium. Those not slain outright are overcome with a smothering inertia, divorcing them from the warp's roiling emotions, as well as denying the most vivid sensations of the physical realm - an agony that particularly pains the daemonic minions of Slaanesh.

Model with storm bolter or master-crafted storm bolter only. Once per battle, when the bearer shoots with a storm bolter, if the target is a DAEMON or PSYKER, you can choose for it to fire a nullbolt. If you do, you can only make one attack with that weapon, but if it scores a hit, that attack inflicts D3+3 mortal wounds on the target and the attack sequence ends. In addition, if the target was a SLAANESH DAEMON, then until the end of the battle, that unit cannot be selected to fight in the Fight phase until after all other eligible units have done so.

The Plaguebane Tome

This tome contains pages crafted from thin sheets of psychoreactive crystal. Each time one of Nurgle's plague daemons is banished, the details of their particular afflictions are mentally transcribed into its pages, along with rites of purification. When recited aloud, nearby followers of Nurgle find their toxic blades significantly less effective.

- Each time an attack is made against the bearer, your opponent cannot re-roll the wound roll.
- The bearer gains the following ability: '**Plaguebane Tome (Aura):** While an enemy NURGLE unit is within 6" of the bearer, each time a model in that unit makes an attack, your opponent cannot re-roll the wound roll.'

Blade of Armageddon

Recovered from the tainted ashes of an almighty banishment, this weapon is believed to have struck the final blow against one of Khorne's monstrous servants during the First Battle for Armageddon. Carried from that devastated world along with the remains of its bearer, this force halberd's blade still radiates with the ferocious psychic residue of that mighty duel, its ferocious power anathema to the minions of the Blood God to this day.

Model with Nemesis force halberd only. The Blade of Armageddon replaces a Nemesis force halberd and has the following profile:

WEAPON	RANGE	TYPE	S	AP	D
Blade of Armageddon	Melee	Melee	+3	-3	3

Abilities: Each time an attack is made with this weapon against a KHORNE DAEMON unit, that attack has a Strength characteristic of x2 and invulnerable saving throws cannot be made against that attack.

Psybane Hood

This psychic hood focuses its power through shards of crystal stolen from Tzeentch's labyrinthine dimension, then sanctified in the Chambers of Purity. Minions of the God of Sorcery find their warp-spawned powers dimmed by the psychic might of those with the strength to wear this relic in battle.

GREY KNIGHTS LIBRARIAN model only. Replace the bearer's Psychic Hood ability with the following: '**Psybane Hood:** Each time a Deny the Witch test is taken for this model, if the unit attempting to manifest the psychic power is within 18" of this model, add 1 to that Deny the Witch test. If the unit attempting to manifest the psychic power is within 18" of this model and is a TZEENTCH DAEMON, add 3 to that Deny the Witch test instead.'

LEGENDARY RELICS

A GREY KNIGHTS CHARACTER of Legendary rank can be given the following Legendary Relic instead of one of the ones presented in the Warhammer 40,000 Core Book. In addition, in order to give a model a Legendary Relic, you must also pay 1 Requisition point (if you do not have enough Requisition points, you cannot give that model a Legendary Relic). Add 2 to a unit's total Crusade points for each Legendary Relic it has – this is in addition to the +1 from gaining a Battle Honour, for a total of +3.

The Helm of Janus

It is unknown if this helmet was once worn by the first Supreme Grand Master himself, for psychic interrogation of its oldest spiritual imprints reveal the paradox of more than one original owner. Via archeotech auto-archival systems, the helm has catalogued every catechism learned by the Chapter over millennia, allowing the wearer to combat the daemonic with a barrage of arcane rituals.

- The bearer knows all of the Psychic powers from the Dominus discipline (pg 64) in addition to any other powers it knows.
- The bearer can attempt to manifest one additional psychic power in your Psychic phase, and can attempt to deny one additional psychic power in your opponent's Psychic phase.

BATTLE TRAITS

When a **GREY KNIGHTS** unit gains a Battle Trait, you can use one of the tables below. If you do, roll one D6 and consult the appropriate table to randomly determine what Battle Trait the unit gains, or choose a Battle Trait from the appropriate table that tells the best narrative for your unit. All the normal rules for Battle Traits apply (e.g. a unit cannot have the same Battle Trait more than once). As with any Battle Honour, make a note on the unit's Crusade card when it gains a Battle Trait and increase its Crusade points accordingly, as described in the Warhammer 40,000 Core Book.

GREY KNIGHTS TERMINATOR UNITS ONLY

D6	TRAIT
1	**Charged Locomotors** *These warriors channel a portion of their psychic consciousness into their armours' artificial muscle bundles.* If this unit successfully manifests a psychic power, then until the end of the turn you can re-roll charge rolls made for this unit.
2	**Punishing Volleys** *Crystalline weapon linkages allow these warriors to effortlessly charge their shots with blasts of psychic power.* If you use the Psybolt Ammunition Stratagem (pg 61) when this unit shoots, reduce the cost by 1CP.
3	**Dominion Blades** *These warriors' weapons shine brightly as they slip efficiently through even the thickest of hides.* Each time this unit successfully manifests the Hammerhand psychic power (pg 65), until the start of your next Psychic phase, improve the Armour Penetration characteristic of Nemesis weapons that models in this unit are equipped with by 1.
4	**Locus of Power (Aura)** *These warriors act as a psychic lodestone for their brethren, boosting their abilities and anchoring the battle line.* While a friendly <**BROTHERHOOD**> **CORE** unit is within 6" of this unit, each time that unit successfully manifests the *Smite* psychic power, you can re-roll the dice to determine the number of mortal wounds inflicted.
5	**Indomitable Bastions** *These warriors project their will as a field of psychic energy, destroying lighter projectiles before they reach them.* Each time an attack with an Armour Penetration characteristic of -1 is allocated to a model in this unit, that attack has an Armour Penetration characteristic of 0 instead.
6	**Proven Slayers** *These warriors are the best of even their elite brotherhood.* Once per battle, if you use the Steel Heart Stratagem (pg 58) when this unit is selected to shoot or fight, it costs 0 Command points instead of 1.

GREY KNIGHTS APOTHECARY UNITS ONLY

D6	TRAIT
1-3	**Spiritual Restoration** *Utilising his potent psychic powers, this healer purges any corruption from the wounds of his allies.* If this model is part of your Crusade army, and if it has not been taken out of action during a battle, then at the end of the battle you can ignore one failed Out of Action test taken for a **GREY KNIGHTS** unit (excluding **VEHICLE** units) — that test is treated as having been passed instead.
4-6	**Battlefield Healer** *An expert at the administration of restoratives, this healer can ensure his brothers are returned to the battle quickly.* Each time you use the Chirurgic Resurrection Stratagem (pg 59), if you select this model, you can roll one D6. On a 4+, gain 1 Command point.

GREY KNIGHTS TECHMARINE UNITS ONLY

D6	TRAIT
1-3	**Machine Spirit Healer** *This warrior ensures the continued purity of the machine's systems in the face of even the greatest corruption.* Each time this model successfully manifests a Psychic power, you can select one **GREY KNIGHTS VEHICLE** model that is within 6" of it. That model regains 1 lost wound.
4-6	**Master of the Motive Force** *Using his psychic abilities to aid repairs, this Techmarine ensures his charges are maintained at peak effectiveness.* If this model is part of your Crusade army, and if it has not been taken out of action during a battle, then at the end of the battle you can ignore one failed Out of Action test taken for a **GREY KNIGHTS VEHICLE** unit — that test is treated as having been passed instead.

GREY KNIGHTS MACHINE SPIRIT UNITS ONLY

D6	TRAIT
1-2	**Aggressive Machine Spirit** *This machine spirit seeks to grind its foes beneath it.* Improve this model's Weapon Skill characteristic by 3.
3-4	**Precise Machine Spirit** *Even under duress, the attacks of this machine remain pinpoint accurate.* This model does not suffer the penalty incurred to its hit rolls for firing at enemy units that are within Engagement Range of it.
5-6	**Indomitable Machine Spirit** *This machine spirit's indomitable might is legendary.* Add 2 to this model's Wounds characteristic.

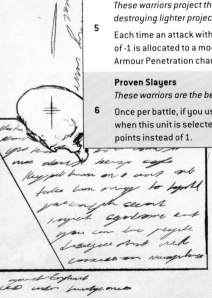

Strike Squad Cytanus heed the calm, mechanical voice of Venerable Gorion, as the daemon world of Threlcinax pulses with a planetary heartbeat of ferocious anger, the rage of Khorne's bloodthirsty minions seeping into the planetary core.

PSYCHIC FORTITUDES

When a **GREY KNIGHTS PSYKER** unit gains a Psychic Fortitude, you can use one of the tables below. If you do, roll one D6 and consult the appropriate table to randomly determine what Psychic Fortitude the unit gains, or choose a Battle Trait from the appropriate table that tells the best narrative for your unit. All the normal rules for Psychic Fortitudes apply (e.g. a unit cannot have the same Psychic Fortitude more than once). As with any Psychic Fortitude, make a note on the unit's Crusade card when it gains a Battle Trait and increase its Crusade points accordingly, as described in the Warhammer 40,000 Core Book.

GREY KNIGHTS CHARACTER UNITS ONLY

D6	TRAIT
1-2	**Malleus Daemonica** *When surrounded by their immortal foes, this warrior's mental powers are enhanced by his manifested hatred and determination.* While this unit is within 6" of any enemy **DAEMON** units, if the Psychic Channelling Stratagem (pg 58) is used when this unit attempts to manifest a psychic power, it costs 0 Command points instead of 1.
3-4	**Focused Might** *The very act of channelling the energies of the empyrean through their body enhances this warrior's already prodigious might.* If this model successfully manifests any psychic powers in your Psychic phase, then until the end of the turn, add 1 to this model's Strength characteristic.
5-6	**Mental Projection** *The warrior's connection to his brothers is so great that he can channel his powers through them, aiding them in their moment of need.* Each time this unit manifests a psychic power from the Dominus discipline, you can select one friendly **GREY KNIGHTS** model within 12" of this model. Measure any distances and check visibility from that model instead.

GREY KNIGHTS NON-CHARACTER UNITS ONLY

D6	TRAIT
1-2	**Fortress of Minds** *Each of these warriors is of such purity that, once gathered together and focusing their powers, there are few malevolent entities that can overwhelm them.* While this unit contains between 5 and 9 models, add 1 to Deny the Witch tests taken for this unit. While this unit contains 10 or more models, add 2 to Deny the Witch tests taken for this unit.
3-4	**Channelled Fury** *The depth of hatred these battle-brothers reserve for their warp-spawned enemies is such that each of their psychic barrages is delivered with overwhelming force, blasting any who would attempt to stop them.* Each time this unit attempts to manifest the *Smite* psychic power, if an enemy **PSYKER** attempts to deny that power and is unsuccessful, that enemy **PSYKER** suffers 1 mortal wound.
5-6	**Layered Minds** *These warriors are trained to overlap their minds while performing rituals, some warriors lashing out with their powers to protect their brothers while the others focus on the task at hand.* While this unit contains 5 or more models, it can attempt to manifest the *Smite* psychic power in the same phase as it performs a psychic action.

DAEMONIC NEMESIS

CREATING YOUR NEMESIS

If your Crusade force includes any **Grey Knights Character** units (other than named characters or characters who have previously had a daemonic nemesis), you can select one of them and create a daemonic nemesis for them. Only one **Grey Knights Character** unit from your Order of Battle can have a daemonic nemesis at a time. That model gains the **Nemesis Hunter** keyword.

Select one of the following units to be the daemonic nemesis:

- **Master of Possession**
- **Herald of Slaanesh**
- **Herald of Nurgle**
- **Herald of Khorne**
- **Herald of Tzeentch**
- **Daemon Prince**
- **Keeper of Secrets**
- **Great Unclean One**
- **Bloodthirster**
- **Lord of Change**

You can select any unit with the listed keyword that is not a named character. Create a Crusade card for the selected unit, including any options that unit may have. Next, select one Battle Honour for your nemesis and record it on its Crusade card. That unit also gains the **Nemesis** keyword, and if it is a **Psyker** it knows the *Smite* psychic power.

The selected unit will be used in several missions over the course of your character's crusade, and its Crusade points total is treated as 0. Each time the **Nemesis Hunter** gains any experience points, the **Nemesis** unit gains the same number of experience points. Each time the **Nemesis** unit gains a rank, select a Battle Honour (or request that your opponent select one) for it as normal and record it on its Crusade card.

HUNTING YOUR NEMESIS

Before each battle, if your opponent's Crusade Faction is **Chaos** and your army includes the **Nemesis Hunter** (and if you or your opponent have the appropriate model), you can roll to determine if the **Nemesis** is present. If the **Nemesis** has a Power Rating of 10 or greater, you can only roll to see if they are present when fighting a Strike Force or Onslaught-sized battle.

To determine whether the **Nemesis** is present, roll one D6, adding 1 to the result if your opponent's army contains any units with the **Chaos Daemons** Faction keyword: on a 5+, the **Nemesis** unit is aiding your opponent, and is added to their army for the battle. This model is ignored when calculating the total Power Level of your opponent's army, cannot be the **Warlord** and cannot perform Actions or gain experience points from any Agendas your opponent selects. This model is not added to any Detachments, and does not prevent other units from their army benefiting from abilities that require every model in an army to have that ability.

The **Nemesis** unit cannot be set up as Reinforcements or Strategic Reserves. If the **Nemesis** unit is a **Psyker**, and your opponent has access to the psychic disciplines it can select from, then in addition to *Smite*, they can select psychic powers for the **Nemesis** unit before the battle, as described on that unit's datasheet. If not, the **Nemesis** unit will only know the *Smite* psychic power as described earlier.

If your opponent's army contains the **Nemesis** unit, they have the following Agenda in addition to any others they can select:

NEFARIOUS SCHEMES!

Bonus Agenda

Though it considers its allies mere tools, the daemon has promised them boons should they aid its malevolent ploys.

At the end of the battle, if the **Nemesis** unit is on the battlefield, you gain 1 additional Requisition point and your **Warlord** gains D3 experience points.

BANISHING YOUR NEMESIS

If the **Nemesis** unit is destroyed, roll 2D6 after the battle and apply the following modifiers:

- If the **Nemesis** unit was destroyed by the **Nemesis Hunter** unit, add 1 to the result.
- If the **Nemesis** unit was destroyed by a melee attack, add 1 to the result.
- For every two True Name points (see below) on your Order of Battle, add 1 to the result.
- If the **Nemesis** unit was destroyed by a ranged attack, subtract 1 from the result.

On an 11+, the **Nemesis** unit is banished. If the **Nemesis** unit is not banished, the nemesis hunter learns a portion of its true name. Gain 1 True Name point. You can keep a record of your True Name points on your Order of Battle. Out of Action tests are never taken for the **Nemesis** unit.

If the **Nemesis** unit is banished, the **Nemesis Hunter** unit gains one Battle Honour. If the **Nemesis** unit was a **Greater Daemon**, the **Nemesis Hunter** unit also gains one Psychic Fortitude. The **Nemesis Hunter** unit then loses the **Nemesis Hunter** keyword and you gain 1 Requisition point. Finally, any True Name points you had collected are lost, and the banished **Nemesis** unit can no longer be used. If you wish, you can select a new **Character** to be the **Nemesis Hunter** and create a new **Nemesis** as described under Creating Your Nemesis, above.

·DEUS·

We saw its influence in the cults on Sorentis, it seemed to peer at us through every tri-horned face mask worn by its puppets. At Caraddin V, it was subtler, three jagged lightning strikes reminding us it watched our purging of the Ghorazon 314th Regiment form. Then at the Strelh Array, it revealed itself and the selfless warrior whose soul it hungered for.

CRUSADE ARMY

This impressive force of Grey Knights belongs to Jason Lee, one of Games Workshop's Security team. An avid collector of miniatures, Jason's Grey Knights form part of a larger force that itself is thematically linked to several of his (many) other armies.

Jason's Grey Knights began as an Armies on Parade project with White Dwarf, and many of his stunning miniatures appear within the magazine's pages. With so many projects on the go at once and several armies painted already, Jason chose to forge his Crusade army from his existing collection, rather than begin a new one. His Grey Knights have a unifying look to them, not only in their armour and weapons, but also in the unusual and incredible bases. The lava effect is repeated from Jason's Salamanders Space Marines – using pieces of broken cork for the rock and Stirland Mud to create ripples of lava. He sees his Grey Knights as having responded to a vision that told of some dark incursion on the Salamanders' fiery planet of Nocturne.

Jason takes his inspiration from a variety of sources including Codexes and novels, and his imagination was especially sparked by Martin Footitt's Golden Demon-winning large-scale Grey Knight from 2007. Jason really wanted to show that his Grey Knights are constantly fighting against the worst horrors the Imperium faces and he likes thinking of them as the elite of the elite. To achieve this, he has given them a battle-worn and gritty feel, carefully painting scuffs and scratches, especially along the business end of their Nemesis force weapons.

Making every model unique in some way is very important to Jason, whether this is done by the way they're posed, painted or even converted – from the armoured sarcophagus of his Dreadnought to the daemon hammer held one-handed by his Interceptor Justicar. He gave every model their own heraldry. In the background, each battle-brother is permitted to display their personal arms. Though this took extra time to do, he considers the final effect well worth the effort. For the superb Grand Master, Jason rebuilt the model's fist using Green Stuff so that his commander is signalling the advance. He rolled Green Stuff into balls to go onto his models' bases. These form bubbles of lava and ensured any left over pieces weren't wasted.

Though he thinks of himself firstly as a collector and then a painter, Jason enjoys pitting his Grey Knights against fellow employees, whether in staff tournaments or in one-off games. He hasn't yet given his Grand Master a name, and jokes that this is because the warrior seems to suffer from terribly poor dice rolls and therefore hasn't 'earned' one in Jason's view. This is despite his generally aggressive play style which he employs not because of game tactics, but because he imagines that's how Grey Knights would fight: heroically pushing forwards and smashing the foe up close! Although maybe, like any good Grey Knight, Jason is keeping the name secret to prevent his daemonic nemeses using it to gain power over him! He's looking forward to expanding the collection with more Terminators and Interceptors, some of his favourite units, but he has other plans, too, and his opponents had better watch out as the force grows.

DATASHEETS

This section contains the datasheets that you will need to fight battles with your Grey Knights miniatures, as well as the weapon profiles for the wargear they can be equipped with. You can find out how to use datasheets and weapon profiles in the Warhammer 40,000 Core Book.

THE <BROTHERHOOD> KEYWORD

The majority of datasheets in this section have the **<BROTHERHOOD>** keyword. This is a keyword that you can select for yourself, as described in the Warhammer 40,000 Core Book, with the guidance detailed below.

With a few notable exceptions, all **GREY KNIGHTS** units are drawn from a brotherhood. When you include such a unit in your army, you must nominate which brotherhood it is from and then replace the **<BROTHERHOOD>** keyword in every instance on its datasheet with the name of your chosen brotherhood. The different Brotherhood keywords you can select from are: **SWORDBEARERS; BLADES OF VICTORY; WARDMAKERS; PRESCIENT BRETHREN; PRESERVERS; RAPIERS; EXACTORS; SILVER BLADES.**

You can find out more about brotherhoods on pages 45-53.

Example: If you include a Grand Master in your army, and you decide he is from the 4th Brotherhood, the Prescient Brethren, his **<BROTHERHOOD>** *keyword becomes* **PRESCIENT BRETHREN** *and his Rites of Battle ability reads 'While a friendly* **PRESCIENT BRETHREN CORE** *unit is within 6" of this model, each time a model in that unit makes an attack, re-roll a hit roll of 1.'*

If your army is Battle-forged, you cannot include units from two different brotherhoods in the same Detachment. You can find out more about Battle-forged armies in the Warhammer 40,000 Core Book.

WARGEAR & WEAPON LISTS

The weapon profiles found on a unit's datasheet describe the primary weapons that models in that unit can be equipped with. Some weapons are only referenced on a datasheet; profiles for these, and all other weapons, can be found on pages 104-107. In addition, some datasheets reference one or more weapon lists (e.g. *Melee Weapons* list); these can be found on page 104.

ABILITIES

A unit's datasheet will list all the abilities it has. Certain abilities that are common to many units are only referenced on the datasheets rather than described in full; these abilities are described below.

KNIGHTS OF TITAN

Grey Knights' skill with bolter and blade is alloyed with their psychic might to create truly formidable warriors.

This unit has the following abilities, which are described below: And They Shall Know No Fear; Bolter Discipline; Masters of the Warp.

And They Shall Know No Fear

Grey Knights face down the darkest horrors that lie beyond the veil of reality, creatures that would shatter the sanity of others.

Each time a Combat Attrition test is taken for this unit, ignore any or all modifiers.

Bolter Discipline

Bolters are holy instruments and symbols of Mankind's power. To the Grey Knights, they are gifts from the Emperor, tools of death that they have mastered to destroy his enemies.

Instead of following the normal rules for Rapid Fire weapons, models in this unit shooting Rapid Fire bolt weapons make double the number of attacks if any of the following apply:

- The shooting model's target is within half the weapon's range.
- The shooting model is **INFANTRY** and its unit Remained Stationary in your previous Movement phase.
- The shooting model is a **TERMINATOR**.

For the purposes of this ability, a Rapid Fire bolt weapon is any bolt weapon (as defined on page 104) with the Rapid Fire type.

DEPLOYMENT ABILITIES

The following abilities, which are used during deployment, are common to many **GREY KNIGHTS** units.

COMBAT SQUADS

Grey Knights squads can break down into tactically flexible formations known as combat squads, while still retaining psychic communion and lethal combat efficacy.

At the start of deployment, before any units have been set up, if this unit contains the maximum number of models that it can, then it can be split into two units containing as equal a number of models as possible. When splitting a unit using this ability, make a note of which models form each of the two new units.

TELEPORT STRIKE

Grey Knights' shrouded strike cruisers and battle barges can teleport their warriors en masse into the very heart of battle, their psychic warriors safe from the warp's insidious touch.

During deployment, if every model in this unit has this ability, then you can set up this unit in a teleportarium chamber instead of setting it up on the battlefield. If you do, then in the Reinforcements step of one of your Movement phases you can set up this unit anywhere on the battlefield that is more than 9" away from any enemy models.

MASTERS OF THE WARP

The Grey Knights wield the warp as a powerful weapon, their purity of soul protecting them from the foul depredations that would strike down lesser men.

If every unit from your army has the GREY KNIGHTS keyword (excluding AGENT OF THE IMPERIUM and UNALIGNED units), PSYKER units with this ability gain a bonus (see below) depending on which Tide of the Warp is dominant for your army, as follows.

At the start of the first battle round, choose which of the Tides is currently dominant. The dominant Tide can subsequently be changed using the *Warp Shaping* psychic power (pg 64).

The available Tides of the Warp are as follows:

TIDE OF CONVERGENCE

The focused energies bound within the Grey Knights' mystical psychic weaponry synchronise with the currents of the empyrean, their lethality surging with the unnatural rhythms of the warp.

While this Tide is dominant for your army:

- Add 6" to the range characteristic of psi weapons (pg 104) that models in this unit are equipped with.
- Each time a model in this unit makes a melee attack with a Nemesis weapon (pg 104), on an unmodified wound roll of 6, the target suffers 1 mortal wound in addition to any normal damage.

TIDE OF CELERITY

Ridden like a howling storm, the warp's power carries the Grey Knights forward at incredible speed as their battle-brothers deftly navigate its ripping currents.

While this Tide is dominant for your army:

- Each time an Advance roll is made for this unit, treat a dice roll of 1-2 as 3 instead.
- Each time a charge roll is made for this unit, treat each dice roll of 1-2 as 3 instead.

TIDE OF SHADOWS

The Grey Knights wreathe themselves in the ever shifting maelstrom of the immaterium, twisting shadow-forms and banks of ethereal mist clouding the minds of those who seek them out.

While this Tide is dominant for your army, each time a ranged attack made by an enemy model more than 12" away from this unit targets this unit, models in this unit are treated as receiving the benefits of Light Cover. If every model in this unit was already receiving the benefits of Light Cover, models in this unit are also treated as receiving the benefits of Dense Cover.

TIDE OF ESCALATION

The roiling tides of the warp swell and heave. Mighty, rushing streams of power flow between the Sons of Titan in a confluence of sorcery that unites their souls in brotherhood, boosting the psykers' ritualistic powers.

While this Tide is dominant for your army, in your Psychic phase, if your army includes any Brotherhood of Psykers Detachments, each time this unit is selected to manifest psychic powers, it can attempt to manifest its brotherhood psychic power, even if that power has already been attempted to be manifested by another unit that phase. Each time such a unit attempts to manifest such a power, then until the end of the phase, add 1 to that power's warp charge value for each other attempt that has been made to manifest it by a unit from your army that phase, whether the attempt was successful or not.

TIDE OF BANISHMENT

All Grey Knights are rigorously trained and conditioned to fight against their daemonic foes. Such is their power and psychic mastery that the Sons of Titan can turn the fickle eddies of the warp itself against the very creatures it nourishes.

While this Tide is dominant for your army:

- This unit gains the following ability: '**Banishment (Aura):** While an enemy DAEMON unit is within 6" of this unit, subtract 2 from the Leadership characteristic of models in that enemy unit.'
- Each time a model in this unit makes an attack against a DAEMON unit, re-roll a hit roll of 1 and re-roll a wound roll of 1.

KALDOR DRAIGO

9 POWER

No.	Name	M	WS	BS	S	T	W	A	Ld	Sv
1	Kaldor Draigo	5"	2+	2+	4	4	7	6	9	2+

Kaldor Draigo is equipped with: The Titansword; Sanctum Sigilum; master-crafted storm bolter; frag grenades; krak grenades.
Your army can only include one KALDOR DRAIGO model.

WEAPON	RANGE	TYPE	S	AP	D	ABILITIES
Master-crafted storm bolter	24"	Rapid Fire 2	4	-1	2	-
The Titansword	Melee	Melee	+4	-4	3	-

OTHER WARGEAR

Sanctum Sigilum	This model has a 3+ invulnerable save.

ABILITIES

Knights of Titan, Teleport Strike (pg 80)

Rites of Battle (Aura): While a friendly GREY KNIGHTS CORE unit is within 6" of this model, each time a model in that unit makes an attack, re-roll a hit roll of 1.

Supreme Grand Master: In your Command phase, select one friendly GREY KNIGHTS CORE or GREY KNIGHTS CHARACTER unit within 6" of this model. Until the start of your next Command phase, each time a model in that unit makes an attack, you can re-roll the hit roll.

PSYKER

This model can attempt to manifest two psychic powers in your Psychic phase and attempt to deny two psychic powers in your opponent's Psychic phase. It knows *Smite* and three psychic powers from the Dominus discipline (pg 64).

FACTION KEYWORDS: IMPERIUM, SANCTIC ASTARTES, GREY KNIGHTS
KEYWORDS: INFANTRY, CHARACTER, PSYKER, PSYK-OUT GRENADES, SUPREME GRAND MASTER, TERMINATOR, HONOURED KNIGHT, KALDOR DRAIGO

The Supreme Grand Master of the Grey Knights, Lord Kaldor Draigo enters battle directly from the warp itself and his resolute spirit inspires his warriors to acts of high valour. He hunts down and slays the spawn of Chaos with psychic fire and blows from the legendary Titansword, its blade reforged with a purified daemon weapon.

'I was there, brothers. At Peraglion, when fate sought to grind us between its palms, when the ground and the sky ruptured and the Hosts Infernus poured out in a vile flood, the Chapter Lord was suddenly there; they were a sea of blackest evil and he an island aflame in their midst.'

- Justicar Qerentis, 2nd Brotherhood, the Peraglion Eradication

'We did not know where the warrior had come from. We felt the haze of warp transla[...], but no teleportation signature, no cipher-sending from the fleet. He bore a panoply that, had I not known better, would have marked him in my eyes as a Grand Master. But we did not know his face, and we d[...] t know his aura. We saw his intent, though, when he cleaved through [...] spawn we fought. With the brother at our side – aye, I name him brother – we cast down the insane prophet and banished those he had summoned. Yet with the sealing of [...], our brother's spirit was pulled from our sight. To this day I do not know who he was.'

- Brother He'nemann, Unknown Brotherhoodafter the Cleansing of Jostero [compiled from fragments of the Stellardell Index]

'He appeared to me, as I know now he appeared to others of the Council. I had not personally witnessed his manifestation for some years, but there was nothing to tell of his exhaustive trials wherever it was the immaterium swept him each time. If anything, he appeared more substantial than at at any time since the curse fell upon him, more vital, more urgent. He sought my counsel on the matter that has haunted the whole Council of late. I gave my lord what he sought, baring my soul in frank admission. This strategy he mulls over, I wonder now whether the author of the Terminus Decree would concur.'

- Grand Master Rothwyr Morvans Protector of the Sanctum Sanctorum, the Era Indomitus'

GRAND MASTER VOLDUS

8 POWER

No.	Name	M	WS	BS	S	T	W	A	Ld	Sv
1	Grand Master Voldus	5"	2+	2+	4	4	6	6	9	2+

Grand Master Voldus is equipped with: master-crafted storm bolter; Malleus Argyrum; frag grenades; krak grenades.
Your army can only include one VOLDUS model.

WEAPON	RANGE	TYPE	S	AP	D	ABILITIES
Master-crafted storm bolter	24"	Rapid Fire 2	4	-1	2	-
Malleus Argyrum	Melee	Melee	x2	-3	3	-

ABILITIES

Knights of Titan, Teleport Strike (pg 80)

Iron Halo: This model has a 4+ invulnerable save.

Rites of Battle (Aura): While a friendly **WARDMAKERS CORE** unit is within 6" of this model, each time a model in that unit makes an attack, re-roll a hit roll of 1.

PSYKER

This model can attempt to manifest two psychic powers in your Psychic phase, and attempt to deny two psychic powers in your opponent's Psychic phase. It knows *Smite* and three psychic powers from the Dominus discipline (pg 64).

FACTION KEYWORDS: IMPERIUM, SANCTIC ASTARTES, GREY KNIGHTS, WARDMAKERS.
KEYWORDS: INFANTRY, CHARACTER, PSYKER, PSYK-OUT GRENADES, GRAND MASTER, TERMINATOR, GRAND MASTER VOLDUS

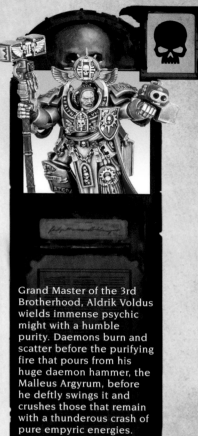

Grand Master of the 3rd Brotherhood, Aldrik Voldus wields immense psychic might with a humble purity. Daemons burn and scatter before the purifying fire that pours from his huge daemon hammer, the Malleus Argyrum, before he deftly swings it and crushes those that remain with a thunderous crash of pure empyric energies.

GRAND MASTER

8 POWER

No.	Name	M	WS	BS	S	T	W	A	Ld	Sv
1	Grand Master	5"	2+	2+	4	4	6	6	9	2+

A Grand Master is equipped with: master-crafted storm bolter; Nemesis force halberd; frag grenades; krak grenades.

WEAPON	RANGE	TYPE	S	AP	D	ABILITIES
Master-crafted storm bolter	24"	Rapid Fire 2	4	-1	2	-
Nemesis force halberd	Melee	Melee	+2	-2	2	-

WARGEAR OPTIONS

- This model's Nemesis force halberd can be replaced with 1 weapon from the *Melee Weapons* list.
- This model's master-crafted storm bolter can be replaced with 1 weapon from the *Special Weapons* list.

ABILITIES

Knights of Titan, Teleport Strike (pg 80)

Iron Halo: This model has a 4+ invulnerable save.

Rites of Battle (Aura): While a friendly <BROTHERHOOD> CORE unit is within 6" of this model, each time a model in that unit makes an attack, re-roll a hit roll of 1.

PSYKER

This model can attempt to manifest one psychic power in your Psychic phase, and attempt to deny one psychic power in your opponent's Psychic phase. It knows *Smite* and two psychic powers from the Dominus discipline (pg 64).

FACTION KEYWORDS: IMPERIUM, SANCTIC ASTARTES, GREY KNIGHTS, <BROTHERHOOD>
KEYWORDS: INFANTRY, CHARACTER, PSYKER, PSYK-OUT GRENADES, TERMINATOR, GRAND MASTER

Grand Masters lead the Grey Knights brotherhoods. Each is a master strategist, a deadly warrior and a terrifying battle-psyker possessed of unhallowed knowledge. Under a Grand Master's guiding will are the unending wars against their daemonic adversaries prosecuted, their stainless souls a beacon of purity.

GRAND MASTER IN NEMESIS DREADKNIGHT   10 POWER

Some of this model's characteristics change as it suffers damage, as shown below:

No.	Name	M	WS	BS	S	T	W	A	Ld	Sv
1	Grand Master in Nemesis Dreadknight (7+ wounds remaining)	9"	2+	2+	6	6	13	6	9	2+
	Grand Master in Nemesis Dreadknight (4-6 wounds remaining)	7"	2+	3+	6	6	N/A	5	9	2+
	Grand Master in Nemesis Dreadknight (1-3 wounds remaining)	5"	2+	4+	6	6	N/A	4	9	2+

A Grand Master in Nemesis Dreadknight is equipped with: 2 dreadfists.

WEAPON	RANGE	TYPE	S	AP	D	ABILITIES
Gatling psilencer	24"	Heavy 12	5	-1	1	-
Heavy incinerator	12"	Heavy 2D6	6	-1	1	Each time an attack is made with this weapon, that attack automatically hits the target.
Heavy psycannon	24"	Heavy 6	8	-2	2	-
Dreadfist	Melee	Melee	x2	-3	2	-
Nemesis daemon greathammer	Melee	Melee	x2	-4	D3+3	Each time an attack is made with this weapon, subtract 1 from that attack's hit roll.
Nemesis greatsword	Before selecting targets, select one of the profiles below to make attacks with.					
- Mighty strike	Melee	Melee	+4	-3	D6	-
- Sweeping blow	Melee	Melee	User	-2	2	Make 2 hit rolls for each attack made with this profile, instead of 1.

OTHER WARGEAR

Dreadknight teleporter	The bearer has the **TELEPORTER** keyword.

WARGEAR OPTIONS

- This model can be equipped with up to two of the following (the same option cannot be selected twice): 1 heavy incinerator; 1 gatling psilencer; 1 heavy psycannon.
- One of this model's dreadfists can be replaced with one of the following: 1 Nemesis daemon greathammer; 1 Nemesis greatsword.
- This model can be equipped with 1 Dreadknight teleporter.

ABILITIES

Knights of Titan, Teleport Strike (pg 80)

Force Shielding: This model has a 4+ invulnerable save.

Rites of Battle (Aura): While a friendly <**BROTHERHOOD**> **CORE** unit is within 6" of this model, each time a model in that unit makes an attack, re-roll a hit roll of 1.

PSYKER

This model can attempt to manifest one psychic power in your Psychic phase, and attempt to deny one psychic power in your opponent's Psychic phase. It knows *Smite* and two psychic powers from the Dominus discipline (pg 64).

FACTION KEYWORDS: **IMPERIUM, SANCTIC ASTARTES, GREY KNIGHTS, <BROTHERHOOD>**
KEYWORDS: **VEHICLE, CHARACTER, PSYKER, NEMESIS DREADKNIGHT, GRAND MASTER**

When they deploy to battle clad in the raiment of a Nemesis Dreadknight, Grand Masters are capable of duelling the greatest daemon lords on an equal footing. Thus girded, their psychic prowess and tactical acumen are wielded alongside the exceptional physical might of a towering and warded Dreadknight suit.

CASTELLAN CROWE

5 POWER

No.	Name	M	WS	BS	S	T	W	A	Ld	Sv
1	Castellan Crowe	6"	2+	2+	4	4	5	6	8	2+

Castellan Crowe is equipped with: storm bolter; Black Blade of Antwyr; frag grenades; krak grenades. Your army can only include one **CASTELLAN CROWE** model.

WEAPON	RANGE	TYPE	S	AP	D	ABILITIES
Storm bolter	24"	Rapid Fire 2	4	0	1	-
Black Blade of Antwyr	Melee	Melee	+1	-3	2	Each time an attack is made with this weapon, an unmodified wound roll of 6 inflicts D3 mortal wounds on the target in addition to any normal damage.

ABILITIES

Knights of Titan, Teleport Strike (pg 80)

Heroic Sacrifice: If this model is destroyed in the Fight phase, do not remove this model from play – it can fight after the attacking model's unit has finished making attacks. If you are using this ability, after resolving this model's attacks, it is then removed.

Iron Halo: This model has a 4+ invulnerable save.

Cleansing Flame: Each time this unit attempts to manifest the *Purifying Flame* psychic power (pg 65), add 1 to that attempt's Psychic test.

Martial Superiority: At the start of the Fight phase, if this model is within Engagement Range of any enemy **CHARACTER** units, it can fight first that phase.

Honour or Death: This model is eligible to perform a Heroic Intervention if it is within 6" horizontally and 5" vertically of any enemy unit, instead of 3" horizontally and 5" vertically. Each time this model makes a Heroic Intervention move, so long as it ends that move either closer to the closest enemy unit or within Engagement Range of an enemy **CHARACTER** unit, it can move up to 6". All other rules for Heroic Interventions still apply.

PSYKER

This model can attempt to manifest one psychic power in your Psychic phase, and attempt to deny one psychic power in your opponent's Psychic phase. It knows *Smite*, one psychic power from the Dominus discipline (pg 64) and *Purifying Flame* from the Sanctic discipline (pg 65).

FACTION KEYWORDS: IMPERIUM, SANCTIC ASTARTES, GREY KNIGHTS, PURIFIER
KEYWORDS: INFANTRY, CHARACTER, PSYKER, PSYK-OUT GRENADES, HONOURED KNIGHT, CASTELLAN CROWE

Castellan Garran Crowe is the Champion of the Order of Purifiers; and his flawless soul radiates outward in a searing, psychic aura. He is the keeper of the Black Blade of Antwyr, a daemon sword that whispers promises and threats. Crowe rejects the blade's vileness, trusting to his masterful combat prowess.

Castellan Garran Crowe rammed his elbow guard into the traitor's helmet and the faceplate cracked, driving slivers of ceramite and bone deep. Crowe swept under the thrusts of his reeling foe's chainsword with a double-handed strike. His blade cut through the archaic power armour and into the corrupted meat and fused ribcage within. Burning gobbets of liquefied armour sizzled and spat from the wound as Crowe pulled the smoking sword free. His actions were calm and controlled, his mind rigid and his priorities clear.

Your soul will burn! You will suffer the agonies of the damned – it is foreseen!

The scream in Crowe's head raged, directionless and impotent against the psychic defences of his mind. He had never sensed it coming directly from the daemon blade itself, but rather as a cloying shadow – ever beaten back by the purity of his soul, but never absent.

You will be peeled apart piece by piece, remade in pleasing form to dance for the Gods of the Neverborn!

Crowe swept on, his brother Purifiers a stride behind him. He sliced open the throat of another Chaos-worshipping Space Marine, the arc of the Black Blade leaving trails of dark flame and warp-tinged vapour. The blade's stream of curses scraped across his consciousness, its frustration and spite pulsing through the weapon as Crowe eviscerated another heretic.

Suddenly solemn and serious, the disembodied voice spoke with a rare clarity.

Your deeds are worthless, Garran. You will fail.

Crowe did not respond. The loathsome daemon was a thing of the warp, capable of knowing many things to come, and yet all it could speak were lies.

A valorous and duty-bound leader, Brother-Captain Arvann Stern has survived battles so brutal often he and his nemesis are the last standing. His growing understanding of the weaknesses of warp-spawn makes his presence anathema to Daemonkind and he wields his Nemesis blade with a furious skill that few can match.

BROTHER-CAPTAIN STERN

6 POWER

No.	Name	M	WS	BS	S	T	W	A	Ld	Sv
1	Brother-Captain Stern	5"	2+	2+	4	4	6	6	9	2+

Brother-Captain Stern is equipped with: master-crafted storm bolter; Nemesis force sword; frag grenades; krak grenades. Your army can only include one **BROTHER-CAPTAIN STERN** model.

WEAPON	RANGE	TYPE	S	AP	D	ABILITIES
Master-crafted storm bolter	24"	Rapid Fire 2	4	-1	2	-
Nemesis force sword	Melee	Melee	+1	-3	2	-

ABILITIES

Knights of Titan, Teleport Strike (pg 80)

The Strands of Fate: In your turn, you can re-roll one hit roll, wound roll or saving throw for this model. If you do, in their next turn your opponent can re-roll one hit roll, wound roll or saving throw for a model in their army.

Iron Halo: This model has a 4+ invulnerable save.

Tactical Precision (Aura): While a friendly **WARDMAKERS CORE** unit is within 6" of this model, each time a model in that unit makes an attack, re-roll a wound roll of 1.

Zone of Banishment: Each time this model successfully manifests a psychic power, each **DAEMON** unit within 6" suffers 1 mortal wound.

PSYKER

This model can attempt to manifest one psychic power in your Psychic phase, and attempt to deny one psychic power in your opponent's Psychic phase. It knows *Smite* and one psychic power from the Dominus discipline (pg 64).

FACTION KEYWORDS: **IMPERIUM, SANCTIC ASTARTES, GREY KNIGHTS, WARDMAKERS**
KEYWORDS: **INFANTRY, CHARACTER, PSYKER, PSYK-OUT GRENADES, BROTHER-CAPTAIN, TERMINATOR, BROTHER-CAPTAIN STERN**

Amongst the Chapter's foremost combatants, a Brother-Captain has proven his worth as a leader of great warriors and a martial exemplar. His place is at the heart of the fight, standing beside his battle-brothers and focusing their blows by means of psychic communion even amidst the din of hellish war.

BROTHER-CAPTAIN

6 POWER

No.	Name	M	WS	BS	S	T	W	A	Ld	Sv
1	Brother-Captain	5"	2+	2+	4	4	6	5	9	2+

A Brother-Captain is equipped with: master-crafted storm bolter; Nemesis force sword; frag grenades; krak grenades.

WEAPON	RANGE	TYPE	S	AP	D	ABILITIES
Master-crafted storm bolter	24"	Rapid Fire 2	4	-1	2	-
Nemesis force sword	Melee	Melee	+1	-3	2	-

WARGEAR OPTIONS

- This model's Nemesis force sword can be replaced with 1 weapon from the *Melee Weapons* list.
- This model's master-crafted storm bolter can be replaced with 1 weapon from the *Special Weapons* list.

ABILITIES

Knights of Titan, Teleport Strike (pg 80)

Iron Halo: This model has a 4+ invulnerable save.

Tactical Precision (Aura): While a friendly **<BROTHERHOOD> CORE** unit is within 6" of this model, each time a model in that unit makes an attack, re-roll a wound roll of 1.

PSYKER

This model can attempt to manifest one psychic power in your Psychic phase, and attempt to deny one psychic power in your opponent's Psychic phase. It knows *Smite* and one psychic power from the Dominus discipline (pg 64).

FACTION KEYWORDS: **IMPERIUM, SANCTIC ASTARTES, GREY KNIGHTS, <BROTHERHOOD>**
KEYWORDS: **INFANTRY, CHARACTER, PSYKER, PSYK-OUT GRENADES, TERMINATOR, BROTHER-CAPTAIN**

BROTHERHOOD CHAMPION

4 POWER

No.	Name	M	WS	BS	S	T	W	A	Ld	Sv
1	Brotherhood Champion	6"	2+	2+	4	4	4	5	8	2+

A Brotherhood Champion is equipped with: storm bolter; Nemesis force sword; frag grenades; krak grenades.

WEAPON	RANGE	TYPE	S	AP	D	ABILITIES
Storm bolter	24"	Rapid Fire 2	4	0	1	-
Nemesis force sword	Melee	Melee	+1	-3	2	-

ABILITIES

Knights of Titan, Teleport Strike (pg 80)

Iron Halo: This model has a 4+ invulnerable save.

Martial Superiority: At the start of the Fight phase, if this model is within Engagement Range of any enemy **CHARACTER** units, it can fight first that phase.

Honour or Death: This model is eligible to perform a Heroic Intervention if it is within 6" horizontally and 5" vertically of any enemy unit, instead of 3" horizontally and 5" vertically. Each time this model makes a Heroic Intervention move, so long as it ends that move either closer to the closest enemy unit or within Engagement Range of an enemy **CHARACTER** unit, it can move up to 6". All other rules for Heroic Interventions still apply.

PSYKER

This model can attempt to manifest one psychic power in your Psychic phase, and attempt to deny one psychic power in your opponent's Psychic phase. It knows *Smite* and one psychic power from the Dominus discipline (pg 64).

FACTION KEYWORDS: **IMPERIUM, SANCTIC ASTARTES, GREY KNIGHTS, <BROTHERHOOD>**
KEYWORDS: **INFANTRY, CHARACTER, PSYKER, PSYK-OUT GRENADES, BROTHERHOOD CHAMPION**

A Brotherhood Champion acts as an exemplar of martial prowess to which all Grey Knights aspire. He is a warrior of peerless skill who mentors new recruits in the ways of the blade. Upon the battlefield, he defends the lives of others and upholds the honour of his brotherhood with deadly skill.

BROTHERHOOD LIBRARIAN

6 POWER

No.	Name	M	WS	BS	S	T	W	A	Ld	Sv
1	Brotherhood Librarian	5"	3+	3+	4	4	5	4	9	2+

A Brotherhood Librarian is equipped with: Nemesis warding stave; frag grenades; krak grenades.

WEAPON	RANGE	TYPE	S	AP	D	ABILITIES
Nemesis warding stave	Melee	Melee	+3	-1	2	-

WARGEAR OPTIONS

- This model's Nemesis warding stave can be replaced with 1 weapon from the *Melee Weapons* list.
- This model can be equipped with one of the following: 1 storm bolter; 1 weapon from the *Combi-weapons* list.

ABILITIES

Knights of Titan, Teleport Strike (pg 80)

Crux Terminatus: This model has a 5+ invulnerable save.

Psychic Hood: Each time a Deny the Witch test is taken for this model, if the unit attempting to manifest the psychic power is within 12" of this model, add 1 to that Deny the Witch test.

PSYKER

This model can attempt to manifest two psychic powers in your Psychic phase, and attempt to deny one psychic power in your opponent's Psychic phase. It knows *Smite* and two psychic powers from either the Dominus and/or Sanctic disciplines (pg 64-65).

FACTION KEYWORDS: **IMPERIUM, SANCTIC ASTARTES, GREY KNIGHTS, <BROTHERHOOD>**
KEYWORDS: **INFANTRY, CHARACTER, PSYKER, PSYK-OUT GRENADES, TERMINATOR, BROTHERHOOD LIBRARIAN**

Librarians have a strength of mind greater even than many of the powerful battle-psykers with whom they fight. The breadth of their empyric scholarship is vast and they courageously brave the deeper and more dangerous reaches of the warp, using psychic rites to shield their fellows or tear at daemonic forms.

BROTHERHOOD TECHMARINE

4 POWER

No.	Name	M	WS	BS	S	T	W	A	Ld	Sv
1	Brotherhood Techmarine	6"	3+	2+	4	4	4	4	8	2+

A Brotherhood Techmarine is equipped with: boltgun; flamer; plasma cutter; Omnissian power axe; 2 servo-arms; frag grenades; krak grenades.

WEAPON	RANGE	TYPE	S	AP	D	ABILITIES
Boltgun	24"	Rapid Fire 1	4	0	1	-
Flamer	12"	Assault D6	4	0	1	Each time an attack is made with this weapon, that attack automatically hits the target.
Plasma cutter		Before selecting targets, select one of the profiles below to make attacks with.				
- Standard	12"	Assault 1	7	-3	1	-
- Supercharge	12"	Assault 1	8	-3	2	If any unmodified hit rolls of 1 are made for attacks with this weapon profile, the bearer is destroyed after shooting with this weapon.
Omnissian power axe	Melee	Melee	+2	-2	2	-
Servo-arm	Melee	Melee	x2	-2	3	Each time the bearer fights, no more than one attack can be made with each servo-arm.

WARGEAR OPTIONS

• This model's boltgun can be replaced with 1 bolt pistol.

ABILITIES

Knights of Titan (pg 80)

Blessing of the Omnissiah: At the end of your Movement phase, this model can repair one friendly GREY KNIGHTS VEHICLE model within 3" of it. That VEHICLE model regains up to D3 lost wounds. Each model can only be repaired once per turn.

Awaken the Machine Spirits: In your Command phase, this model can awaken one friendly GREY KNIGHTS VEHICLE model within 3" of it. Until the start of your next Command phase, each time that VEHICLE model makes a ranged attack, add 1 to that attack's hit roll. Each model can only be awakened once per turn.

PSYKER

This model can attempt to manifest one psychic power in your Psychic phase, and attempt to deny one psychic power in your opponent's Psychic phase. It knows *Smite* and one psychic power from the Dominus discipline (pg 64).

FACTION KEYWORDS: IMPERIUM, SANCTIC ASTARTES, GREY KNIGHTS, <BROTHERHOOD>
KEYWORDS: INFANTRY, CHARACTER, PSYKER, PSYK-OUT GRENADES, BROTHERHOOD TECHMARINE

Psychic warrior-smiths with esoteric knowledge of machine mysteries, Techmarines maintain and repair the weapons, armour and mighty vehicles used by the Grey Knights. With mechanical servo-arms, and through the rites of the Omnissiah, they fortify the spirits of wounded machines against the claws of daemons.

BROTHERHOOD CHAPLAIN

6 POWER

No.	Name	M	WS	BS	S	T	W	A	Ld	Sv
1	Brotherhood Chaplain	5"	2+	3+	4	4	5	4	9	2+

A Brotherhood Chaplain is equipped with: storm bolter; crozius arcanum; frag grenades; krak grenades.

WEAPON	RANGE	TYPE	S	AP	D	ABILITIES
Storm bolter	24"	Rapid Fire 2	4	0	1	-
Crozius arcanum	Melee	Melee	+2	-1	2	-

ABILITIES

Knights of Titan, Teleport Strike (pg 80)

Spiritual Leaders (Aura): While a friendly GREY KNIGHTS CORE unit is within 6" of this model, models in that unit can use this model's Leadership characteristic instead of their own.

Rosarius: This model has a 4+ invulnerable save.

PSYKER

This model can attempt to manifest one psychic power in your Psychic phase, and attempt to deny one psychic power in your opponent's Psychic phase. It knows *Smite* and one psychic power from the Dominus discipline (pg 64).

PRIEST

This model knows the *Litany of Expulsion* and one other litany from the Litanies of Purity (pg 66). In your Command phase, if this model is on the battlefield, it can recite one litany it knows that has not already been recited by a friendly model that battle round. Roll one D6: on a 3+, the recited litany is inspiring and takes effect until the start of your next Command phase.

FACTION KEYWORDS: IMPERIUM, SANCTIC ASTARTES, GREY KNIGHTS, <BROTHERHOOD>
KEYWORDS: INFANTRY, CHARACTER, PSYKER, PSYK-OUT GRENADES, PRIEST, TERMINATOR, BROTHERHOOD CHAPLAIN

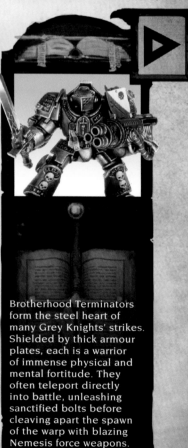

Chaplains intone psychic litanies of sanctity and contempt, speaking the Emperor's word to their brethren in stentorian tones. They are symbols of brutal mortality and unquestioning zeal. In battle, they lay about the foe with blows from their crozius arcanum and with impassioned canticles ward their brothers' souls.

BROTHERHOOD TERMINATOR SQUAD

12 POWER

No.	Name	M	WS	BS	S	T	W	A	Ld	Sv
4-9	Brotherhood Terminator	5"	3+	3+	4	4	3	3	7	2+
1	Terminator Justicar	5"	3+	3+	4	4	3	4	8	2+

If this unit contains 6 or more models, it has **Power Rating 24**. Every model is equipped with: storm bolter; Nemesis force sword; frag grenades; krak grenades.

WEAPON	RANGE	TYPE	S	AP	D	ABILITIES
Storm bolter	24"	Rapid Fire 2	4	0	1	-
Nemesis force sword	Melee	Melee	+1	-3	2	-

WARGEAR OPTIONS

- Any number of models can each have their Nemesis force sword replaced with 1 weapon from the *Melee Weapons* list.
- For every 5 models in this unit, 1 model's storm bolter can be replaced with 1 weapon from the *Special Weapons* list.

ABILITIES

Knights of Titan, Combat Squads, Teleport Strike (pg 80x)

Crux Terminatus: All models in this unit have a 5+ invulnerable save.

PSYKER

This unit can attempt to manifest one psychic power in your Psychic phase, and attempt to deny one psychic power in your opponent's Psychic phase. It knows *Smite,* and *Hammerhand* from the Sanctic discipline (pg 65).

FACTION KEYWORDS: IMPERIUM, SANCTIC ASTARTES, GREY KNIGHTS, <BROTHERHOOD>
KEYWORDS: INFANTRY, CORE, PSYKER, TERMINATOR, PSYK-OUT GRENADES, BROTHERHOOD TERMINATOR SQUAD

Brotherhood Terminators form the steel heart of many Grey Knights' strikes. Shielded by thick armour plates, each is a warrior of immense physical and mental fortitude. They often teleport directly into battle, unleashing sanctified bolts before cleaving apart the spawn of the warp with blazing Nemesis force weapons.

STRIKE SQUAD

6 POWER

No.	Name	M	WS	BS	S	T	W	A	Ld	Sv
4-9	Grey Knight	6"	3+	3+	4	4	2	3	7	3+
1	Justicar	6"	3+	3+	4	4	2	4	8	3+

If this unit contains 6 or more models, it has **Power Rating 12**. Every model is equipped with: storm bolter; Nemesis force sword; frag grenades; krak grenades.

WEAPON	RANGE	TYPE	S	AP	D	ABILITIES
Storm bolter	24"	Rapid Fire 2	4	0	1	-
Nemesis force sword	Melee	Melee	+1	-3	2	-

WARGEAR OPTIONS

- Any number of models can each have their Nemesis force sword replaced with 1 weapon from the *Melee Weapons* list.
- For every 5 models in this unit, 1 Grey Knight's storm bolter and Nemesis force sword can be replaced with 1 weapon from the *Special Weapons* list.

ABILITIES

Knights of Titan, Combat Squads, Teleport Strike (pg 80)

PSYKER

This unit can attempt to manifest one psychic power in your Psychic phase, and attempt to deny one psychic power in your opponent's Psychic phase. It knows *Smite,* and *Hammerhand* from the Sanctic discipline (pg 65).

FACTION KEYWORDS: Imperium, Sanctic Astartes, Grey Knights, <Brotherhood>
KEYWORDS: Infantry, Core, Psyker, Psyk-out Grenades, Strike Squad

Strike Squads often form a vanguard, striking swiftly and slipping through gaps in daemonic lines to seal warp portals or prevent summoners escaping. Frequently attacking from fixed teleportariums or swift transports, they conduct vital reconnaissance, disrupt flanks and blunt incursions with surgical strikes.

BROTHERHOOD APOTHECARY

6 POWER

No.	Name	M	WS	BS	S	T	W	A	Ld	Sv
1	Brotherhood Apothecary	5"	3+	3+	4	4	5	5	8	2+

A Brotherhood Apothecary is equipped with: Nemesis force sword; frag grenades; krak grenades.

WEAPON	RANGE	TYPE	S	AP	D	ABILITIES
Nemesis force sword	Melee	Melee	+1	-3	2	-

WARGEAR OPTIONS

- This model's Nemesis force sword can be replaced with 1 of the following: 1 Nemesis Daemon hammer; 1 Nemesis falchion; 1 Nemesis force halberd; 1 Nemesis force sword; 1 Nemesis warding stave.

ABILITIES

Knights of Titan, Teleport Strike (pg 80)

Crux Terminatus: This model has a 5+ invulnerable save.

Combat Restoratives: At the end of your Movement phase, this model can heal one friendly GREY KNIGHTS INFANTRY model whose unit is within 3" of it. That model regains up to D3 lost wounds. Each model can only be healed once per turn.

Narthecium (Aura): While a friendly GREY KNIGHTS INFANTRY unit is within 3" of this model, each time a model in that unit would lose a wound, roll one D6: on a 6, that wound is not lost.

PSYKER

This model can attempt to manifest one psychic power in your Psychic phase, and attempt to deny one psychic power in your opponent's Psychic phase. It knows *Smite* and one psychic power from the Dominus discipline (pg 64).

FACTION KEYWORDS: IMPERIUM, SANCTIC ASTARTES, GREY KNIGHTS, <BROTHERHOOD>
KEYWORDS: INFANTRY, CHARACTER, PSYKER, PSYK-OUT GRENADES, TERMINATOR, BROTHERHOOD APOTHECARY

Apothecaries have the vital task of ensuring the physical purity of their battle-brothers and healing those who are wounded. These arcane surgeons excise sorcerous bullets and daemon claw splinters from their battle-brothers, purge psychic maladies using their empyric powers or recover the gene-seed of the dead.

BROTHERHOOD ANCIENT

5 POWER

No.	Name	M	WS	BS	S	T	W	A	Ld	Sv
1	Brotherhood Ancient	5"	3+	3+	4	4	5	4	8	2+

A Brotherhood Ancient is equipped with: storm bolter; frag grenades; krak grenades.

WEAPON	RANGE	TYPE	S	AP	D	ABILITIES
Storm bolter	24"	Rapid Fire 2	4	0	1	-
Nemesis falchion	Melee	Melee	User	-2	1	Each time the bearer fights, if it is equipped with one or more Nemesis falchions, it makes 1 additional attack using this profile.

WARGEAR OPTIONS

- This model can be equipped with 1 Nemesis falchion.

ABILITIES

Knights of Titan, Teleport Strike (pg 80)

Crux Terminatus: This model has a 5+ invulnerable save.

Sacred Banner (Aura): While a friendly <BROTHERHOOD> CORE unit is within 6" of this model, add 1 to the Leadership characteristic of models in that unit. In addition, while a friendly <BROTHERHOOD> CORE INFANTRY unit is within 6" of this model, add 1 to the Attacks characteristic of models in that unit.

PSYKER

This model can attempt to manifest one psychic power in your Psychic phase, and attempt to deny one psychic power in your opponent's Psychic phase. It knows *Smite* and one psychic power from the Dominus discipline (pg 64).

FACTION KEYWORDS: IMPERIUM, SANCTIC ASTARTES, GREY KNIGHTS, <BROTHERHOOD>
KEYWORDS: INFANTRY, CHARACTER, PSYKER, PSYK-OUT GRENADES, ANCIENT, TERMINATOR, BROTHERHOOD ANCIENT

Heroic and selfless deeds are honoured by recording them upon sacred banners. These pristine standards are sometimes taken to battle by Brotherhood Ancients, who guard the inspiring relics with their lives. Such banners may depict the banishment of daemons and are powerful inspirations to those who fight in their shadow.

PALADIN SQUAD

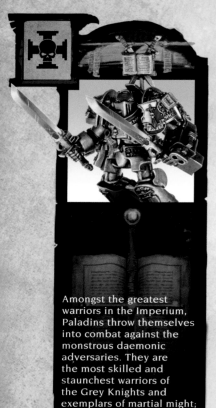

13 POWER

No.	Name	M	WS	BS	S	T	W	A	Ld	Sv
2-9	Paladin	5"	2+	3+	4	4	3	4	8	2+
1	Paragon	5"	2+	3+	4	4	3	5	9	2+

If this unit contains 6 or more models, it has **Power Rating 26**. Every model is equipped with: storm bolter; Nemesis force sword; frag grenades; krak grenades.

WEAPON	RANGE	TYPE	S	AP	D	ABILITIES
Storm bolter	24"	Rapid Fire 2	4	0	1	-
Nemesis force sword	Melee	Melee	+1	-3	2	-

WARGEAR OPTIONS

- Any number of models can each have their Nemesis force sword replaced with 1 weapon from the *Melee Weapons* list.
- For every 5 models in this unit, up to 2 Paladins can each have their storm bolter replaced with 1 weapon from the *Special Weapons* list.

ABILITIES

Knights of Titan, Combat Squads, Teleport Strike (pg 80)   **Crux Terminatus:** All models in this unit have a 5+ invulnerable save.

PSYKER

This unit can attempt to manifest one psychic power in your Psychic phase, and attempt to deny one psychic power in your opponent's Psychic phase. It knows *Smite*, and two psychic powers from the Sanctic discipline (pg 65).

FACTION KEYWORDS: IMPERIUM, SANCTIC ASTARTES, GREY KNIGHTS, PALADIN
KEYWORDS: INFANTRY, CORE, PSYKER, PSYK-OUT GRENADES, TERMINATOR, HONOURED KNIGHT, PALADIN SQUAD

Amongst the greatest warriors in the Imperium, Paladins throw themselves into combat against the monstrous daemonic adversaries. They are the most skilled and staunchest warriors of the Grey Knights and exemplars of martial might; each Paladin has banished one of the most powerful daemons ever to manifest.

PURIFIER SQUAD

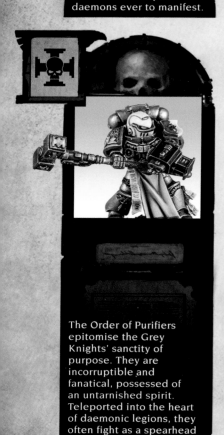

7 POWER

No.	Name	M	WS	BS	S	T	W	A	Ld	Sv
4-9	Purifier	6"	3+	3+	4	4	2	3	8	3+
1	Knight of the Flame	6"	3+	3+	4	4	2	4	9	3+

If this unit contains 6 or more models, it has **Power Rating 14**. Every model is equipped with: storm bolter; Nemesis force sword; frag grenades; krak grenades.

WEAPON	RANGE	TYPE	S	AP	D	ABILITIES
Storm bolter	24"	Rapid Fire 2	4	0	1	-
Nemesis force sword	Melee	Melee	+1	-3	2	-

WARGEAR OPTIONS

- Any number of models can each have their Nemesis force sword replaced with 1 weapon from the *Melee Weapons* list.
- For every 5 models in this unit, up to 2 Purifiers can each have their storm bolter and Nemesis force sword replaced with 1 weapon from the *Special Weapons* list.

ABILITIES

Knights of Titan, Combat Squads, Teleport Strike (pg 80)

Cleansing Flame: Each time this unit attempts to manifest the *Purifying Flame* psychic power (pg 65), add 1 to that attempt's Psychic test.

PSYKER

This unit can attempt to manifest one psychic power in your Psychic phase, and attempt to deny one psychic power in your opponent's Psychic phase. It knows *Smite*, and *Purifying Flame* from the Sanctic discipline (pg 65).

FACTION KEYWORDS: IMPERIUM, SANCTIC ASTARTES, GREY KNIGHTS, PURIFIER
KEYWORDS: INFANTRY, CORE, PSYKER, PSYK-OUT GRENADES, HONOURED KNIGHT, PURIFIER SQUAD

The Order of Purifiers epitomise the Grey Knights' sanctity of purpose. They are incorruptible and fanatical, possessed of an untarnished spirit. Teleported into the heart of daemonic legions, they often fight as a spearhead from where they unleash a cleansing fire that sears the corrupted to ash.

PALADIN ANCIENT

6 POWER

No.	Name	M	WS	BS	S	T	W	A	Ld	Sv
1	Paladin Ancient	5"	2+	3+	4	4	5	5	9	2+

A Paladin Ancient is equipped with: storm bolter; frag grenades; krak grenades. Your army can only include one **PALADIN ANCIENT**.

WEAPON	RANGE	TYPE	S	AP	D	ABILITIES
Storm bolter	24"	Rapid Fire 2	4	0	1	-
Nemesis falchion	Melee	Melee	User	-2	1	Each time the bearer fights, if it is equipped with one or more Nemesis falchions, it makes 1 additional attack using this profile.

WARGEAR OPTIONS

- This model can be equipped with 1 Nemesis falchion.
- If this model is not equipped with 1 Nemesis Falchion, its storm bolter can be replaced with 1 weapon from the *Special Weapons* list.

ABILITIES

Knights of Titan, Teleport Strike (pg 80)

Sacred Banner (Aura): While a friendly **PALADIN CORE** unit is within 6" of this model, add 1 to the Leadership characteristic of models in that unit. In addition, while a friendly **PALADIN CORE INFANTRY** unit is within 6" of this model, add 1 to the Attacks characteristic of models in that unit.

Crux Terminatus: This model has a 5+ invulnerable save.

Chapter Banner: In your Command phase, select one friendly **GREY KNIGHTS CORE** unit within 6" of this model. Until the start of your next Command phase, each time a model in that unit makes a melee attack, add 1 to that attack's hit roll.

PSYKER

This model can attempt to manifest one psychic power in your Psychic phase, and attempt to deny one psychic power in your opponent's Psychic phase. It knows *Smite* and one psychic power from the Dominus discipline (pg 64).

FACTION KEYWORDS: IMPERIUM, SANCTIC ASTARTES, GREY KNIGHTS, PALADIN
KEYWORDS: INFANTRY, CHARACTER, PSYKER, PSYK-OUT GRENADES, TERMINATOR, HONOURED KNIGHT, PALADIN ANCIENT

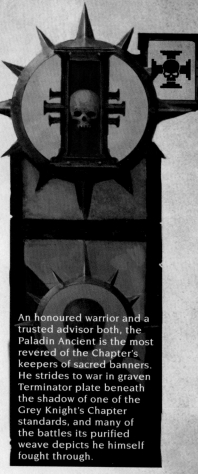

An honoured warrior and a trusted advisor both, the Paladin Ancient is the most revered of the Chapter's keepers of sacred banners. He strides to war in graven Terminator plate beneath the shadow of one of the Grey Knight's Chapter standards, and many of the battles its purified weave depicts he himself fought through.

SERVITORS

2 POWER

No.	Name	M	WS	BS	S	T	W	A	Ld	Sv
4	Servitor	5"	5+	5+	3	3	1	1	6	4+

Every model is equipped with: servo-arm.

WEAPON	RANGE	TYPE	S	AP	D	ABILITIES
Heavy bolter	36"	Heavy 3	5	-1	2	-
Multi-melta	24"	Heavy 2	8	-4	D6	Each time an attack made with this weapon targets a unit within half range, that attack has a Damage characteristic of D6+2.
Plasma cannon	Before selecting targets, select one of the profiles below to make attacks with.					
- Standard	36"	Heavy D3	7	-3	1	Blast
- Supercharge	36"	Heavy D3	8	-3	2	Blast. If any unmodified hit rolls of 1 are made for attacks with this weapon profile, the bearer is destroyed after shooting with this weapon.
Servo-arm	Melee	Melee	x2	-2	3	Each time the bearer fights, no more than one attack can be made with each servo-arm.

WARGEAR OPTIONS

- Up to 2 Servitors can each have their servo-arm replaced with one of the following: 1 heavy bolter; 1 multi-melta; 1 plasma cannon.

ABILITIES

Mindlock: While this unit is within 6" of any friendly **GREY KNIGHTS TECHMARINE** units, models in this unit have a Weapon Skill and Ballistic Skill characteristic of 4+ and a Leadership characteristic of 9. In addition, if your army is Battle-forged, then for each **<BROTHERHOOD> TECHMARINE** unit included in a Detachment, one **<BROTHERHOOD> SERVITORS** unit can be included in that Detachment without taking up a Battlefield Role slot

FACTION KEYWORDS: IMPERIUM, SANCTIC ASTARTES, GREY KNIGHTS, <BROTHERHOOD>
KEYWORDS: INFANTRY, SERVITORS

Some servitors were once serfs, failed aspirants or former allies, now cyborgised with mechanical augmentation. Many have limbs replaced with servo-arms or heavy weapons, employed to defend or aid their Techmarine masters during repairs. The brutal mind-wiping process ensures none ever reveal what they have witnessed.

VENERABLE DREADNOUGHT

8 POWER

No.	Name	M	WS	BS	S	T	W	A	Ld	Sv
1	Venerable Dreadnought	6"	2+	2+	6	7	8	5	8	3+

A Venerable Dreadnought is equipped with: assault cannon; storm bolter; Dreadnought combat weapon.

WEAPON	RANGE	TYPE	S	AP	D	ABILITIES
Assault cannon	24"	Heavy 6	6	-1	1	-
Heavy flamer	12"	Heavy D6	5	-1	1	Each time an attack is made with this weapon, that attack automatically hits the target.
Heavy plasma cannon		Before selecting targets, select one of the profiles below to make attacks with.				
- Standard	36"	Heavy D3	7	-3	2	Blast
- Supercharge	36"	Heavy D3	8	-3	3	Blast. Each time an unmodified hit roll of 1 is made for an attack with this weapon profile, the bearer suffers 1 mortal wound after shooting this weapon.
Missile launcher		Before selecting targets, select one of the profiles below to make attacks with.				
- Frag missile	48"	Heavy D6	4	0	1	Blast
- Krak missile	48"	Heavy 1	8	-2	D6	-
Multi-melta	24"	Heavy 2	8	-4	D6	Each time an attack made with this weapon targets a unit within half range, that attack has a Damage characteristic of D6+2.
Twin lascannon	48"	Heavy 2	9	-3	D6	-
Storm bolter	24"	Rapid Fire 2	4	0	1	-
Dreadnought combat weapon	Melee	Melee	x2	-3	3	-

WARGEAR OPTIONS

- This model's assault cannon can be replaced with one of the following: 1 heavy plasma cannon; 1 multi-melta; 1 twin lascannon.
- This model's Dreadnought combat weapon and storm bolter can be replaced with one of the following:
  - 1 missile launcher.
  - 1 Dreadnought combat weapon and 1 heavy flamer.

ABILITIES

Knights of Titan (pg 80)

Explodes: When this model is destroyed, roll one D6 before removing it from play. On a 6 it explodes, and each unit within 3" suffers 1 mortal wound.

Duty Eternal: Each time an attack is allocated to this model, subtract 1 from the Damage characteristic of that attack (to a minimum of 1).

Unyielding Ancient: Each time this model would lose a wound, roll one D6: on a 6, that wound is not lost.

PSYKER

This model can attempt to manifest one psychic power in your Psychic phase, and attempt to deny one psychic power in your opponent's Psychic phase. It knows *Smite,* and *Armoured Resilience* from the Sanctic discipline (pg 65).

FACTION KEYWORDS: **Imperium, Sanctic Astartes, Grey Knights**
KEYWORDS: **Vehicle, Core, Psyker, Dreadnought, Smokescreen, Honoured Knight, Venerable Dreadnought**

Venerable Dreadnoughts house truly ancient champions whose revered belligerence endures war after war. Their strategic acumen and wisdom of ancient horrors banished in past battles is respectfully sought, but they still take to the battlefield with a stoic resolve, and to fight alongside these living legends is a high honour.

DREADNOUGHT

7 POWER

No.	Name	M	WS	BS	S	T	W	A	Ld	Sv
1	Dreadnought	6"	3+	3+	6	7	8	5	8	3+

A Dreadnought is equipped with: assault cannon; storm bolter; Dreadnought combat weapon.

WEAPON	RANGE	TYPE	S	AP	D	ABILITIES
Assault cannon	24"	Heavy 6	6	-1	1	-
Heavy flamer	12"	Heavy D6	5	-1	1	Each time an attack is made with this weapon, that attack automatically hits the target.
Heavy plasma cannon	Before selecting targets, select one of the profiles below to make attacks with.					
- Standard	36"	Heavy D3	7	-3	2	Blast
- Supercharge	36"	Heavy D3	8	-3	3	Blast. Each time an unmodified hit roll of 1 is made for an attack with this weapon profile, the bearer suffers 1 mortal wound after shooting this weapon.
Missile launcher	Before selecting targets, select one of the profiles below to make attacks with.					
- Frag missile	48"	Heavy D6	4	0	1	Blast
- Krak missile	48"	Heavy 1	8	-2	D6	-
Multi-melta	24"	Heavy 2	8	-4	D6	Each time an attack made with this weapon targets a unit within half range, that attack has a Damage characteristic of D6+2.
Twin lascannon	48"	Heavy 2	9	-3	D6	-
Storm bolter	24"	Rapid Fire 2	4	0	1	-
Dreadnought combat weapon	Melee	Melee	x2	-3	3	-

WARGEAR OPTIONS

- This model's assault cannon can be replaced with one of the following: 1 heavy plasma cannon; 1 multi-melta; 1 twin lascannon.
- This model's Dreadnought combat weapon and storm bolter can be replaced with one of the following:
  - 1 missile launcher.
  - 1 Dreadnought combat weapon and 1 heavy flamer.

ABILITIES

Knights of Titan (pg 80)

Explodes: When this model is destroyed, roll one D6 before removing it from play. On a 6 it explodes, and each unit within 3" suffers 1 mortal wound.

Duty Eternal: Each time an attack is allocated to this model, subtract 1 from the Damage characteristic of that attack (to a minimum of 1).

PSYKER

This model can attempt to manifest one psychic power in your Psychic phase, and attempt to deny one psychic power in your opponent's Psychic phase. It knows *Smite,* and *Armoured Resilience* from the Sanctic discipline (pg 65).

FACTION KEYWORDS: **IMPERIUM, SANCTIC ASTARTES, GREY KNIGHTS, <BROTHERHOOD>**
KEYWORDS: **VEHICLE, CORE, PSYKER, SMOKESCREEN, DREADNOUGHT**

Within a Dreadnought's armoured sarcophagus lie what remains of a mortally wounded hero of the Grey Knights. Even long after falling in the fight against the Ruinous Powers they serve the Chapter, piloting a fearsome combat walker fitted with devastating heavy weapons with which they yet destroy their foes.

INTERCEPTOR SQUAD

7 POWER

No.	Name	M	WS	BS	S	T	W	A	Ld	Sv
4-9	Interceptor	12"	3+	3+	4	4	2	3	7	3+
1	Interceptor Justicar	12"	3+	3+	4	4	2	4	8	3+

If this unit contains 6 or more models, it has **Power Rating 14**. Every model is equipped with: storm bolter; Nemesis force sword; frag grenades; krak grenades.

WEAPON	RANGE	TYPE	S	AP	D	ABILITIES
Storm bolter	24"	Rapid Fire 2	4	0	1	-
Nemesis force sword	Melee	Melee	+1	-3	2	-

WARGEAR OPTIONS

- Any number of models can each have their Nemesis force sword replaced with 1 weapon from the *Melee Weapons* list.
- For every 5 models in this unit, 1 model's storm bolter and Nemesis force sword can be replaced with 1 weapon from the *Special Weapons* list.

ABILITIES

Knights of Titan, Combat Squads, Teleport Strike (pg 80)

Personal Teleporters: Each time this unit makes a Normal Move, Advances, or Falls Back, models in this unit can be moved across other models (and their bases) as if they were not there, and they can be moved within Engagement Range of enemy models. In addition, any vertical distance up and/or down that they make as part of that move is ignored. However, these models cannot finish this move either on top of another model (or its base) or within Engagement Range of any enemy models

PSYKER

This unit can attempt to manifest one psychic power in your Psychic phase, and attempt to deny one psychic power in your opponent's Psychic phase. It knows *Smite,* and *Ethereal Castigation* from the Sanctic discipline (pg 65).

FACTION KEYWORDS: **IMPERIUM, SANCTIC ASTARTES, GREY KNIGHTS, <BROTHERHOOD>**
KEYWORDS: **INFANTRY, CORE, PSYKER, PSYK-OUT GRENADES, TELEPORTER, INTERCEPTOR SQUAD**

Bearing personal teleporters, Interceptors jump across the battlefield in a series of rapid, site-to-site teleportations, redeploying at speed or hunting down swift foes. Arriving in a blaze of light, they turn their weapons and powers on stunned enemies in a storm of death, before vanishing as swiftly as they arrived.

PURGATION SQUAD

6 POWER

No.	Name	M	WS	BS	S	T	W	A	Ld	Sv
4-9	Purgator	6"	3+	3+	4	4	2	3	7	3+
1	Purgator Justicar	6"	3+	3+	4	4	2	4	8	3+

If this unit contains 6 or more models, it has **Power Rating 12**. Every model is equipped with: storm bolter; Nemesis force sword; frag grenades; krak grenades.

WEAPON	RANGE	TYPE	S	AP	D	ABILITIES
Storm bolter	24"	Rapid Fire 2	4	0	1	-
Nemesis force sword	Melee	Melee	+1	-3	2	-

WARGEAR OPTIONS

- Any number of models can each have their Nemesis force sword replaced with 1 weapon from the *Melee Weapons* list.
- Up to four Purgators can each have their storm bolter and Nemesis force sword replaced with 1 weapon from the *Special Weapons* list.

ABILITIES

Knights of Titan, Combat Squads, Teleport Strike (pg 80)

PSYKER

This unit can attempt to manifest one psychic power in your Psychic phase, and attempt to deny one psychic power in your opponent's Psychic phase. It knows *Smite,* and *Astral Aim* from the Sanctic discipline (pg 65).

FACTION KEYWORDS: **IMPERIUM, SANCTIC ASTARTES, GREY KNIGHTS, <BROTHERHOOD>**
KEYWORDS: **INFANTRY, CORE, PSYKER, PSYK-OUT GRENADES, PURGATION SQUAD**

Purgation Squads keep pace with the main attack, supporting their brother knights with fearsome torrents of heavy and arcane weapons fire. Their psychic senses cleave through the warp to discern their foes, enabling seemingly impossible shots that cleanse shadowy lairs and fortified hideaways of daemons.

NEMESIS DREADKNIGHT

8 POWER

Some of this model's characteristics change as it suffers damage, as shown below:

No.	Name	M	WS	BS	S	T	W	A	Ld	Sv
1	Nemesis Dreadknight (7+ wounds remaining)	9"	3+	3+	6	6	13	5	8	2+
	Nemesis Dreadknight (4-6 wounds remaining)	7"	3+	4+	6	6	N/A	4	8	2+
	Nemesis Dreadknight (1-3 wounds remaining)	5"	3+	5+	6	6	N/A	3	8	2+

A Nemesis Dreadknight is equipped with: 2 dreadfists.

WEAPON	RANGE	TYPE	S	AP	D	ABILITIES
Gatling psilencer	24"	Heavy 12	5	-1	1	-
Heavy incinerator	12"	Heavy 2D6	6	-1	1	Each time an attack is made with this weapon, that attack automatically hits the target.
Heavy psycannon	24"	Heavy 6	8	-2	2	-
Dreadfist	Melee	Melee	x2	-3	2	-
Nemesis daemon greathammer	Melee	Melee	x2	-4	D3+3	Each time an attack is made with this weapon, subtract 1 from that attack's hit roll.
Nemesis greatsword	Before selecting targets, select one of the profiles below to make attacks with.					
- Mighty strike	Melee	Melee	+4	-3	D6	-
- Sweeping blow	Melee	Melee	User	-2	2	Make 2 hit rolls for each attack made with this profile, instead of 1.

OTHER WARGEAR

| Dreadknight teleporter | The bearer has the **TELEPORTER** keyword. |

WARGEAR OPTIONS

- This model can be equipped with up to two of the following (the same option cannot be selected twice): 1 gatling psilencer; 1 heavy incinerator; 1 heavy psycannon.
- One of this model's dreadfists can be replaced with one of the following: 1 Nemesis daemon greathammer; 1 Nemesis greatsword.
- This model can be equipped with 1 Dreadknight teleporter.

ABILITIES

Knights of Titan, Teleport Strike (pg 80)

Force Shielding: This model has a 4+ invulnerable save.

PSYKER

This model can attempt to manifest one psychic power in your Psychic phase, and attempt to deny one psychic power in your opponent's Psychic phase. It knows *Smite*, and *Hammerhand* from the Sanctic discipline (pg 65).

FACTION KEYWORDS: IMPERIUM, SANCTIC ASTARTES, GREY KNIGHTS, <BROTHERHOOD>
KEYWORDS: VEHICLE, CORE, PSYKER, NEMESIS DREADKNIGHT

The pilot of a Nemesis Dreadknight commands a towering exoskeleton armoured in thrice-blessed bonded ceramite. Powered by his psychic might, its heavy weapons scythe through warp-spawned hordes, while with giant fists or enlarged force weapons it smashes daemon-infused vehicles and titanic horrors to ruin.

LAND RAIDER

Some of this model's characteristics change as it suffers damage, as shown below:

No.	Name	M	WS	BS	S	T	W	A	Ld	Sv
1	Land Raider (9+ wounds remaining)	10"	6+	3+	8	8	16	6	9	2+
	Land Raider (5-8 wounds remaining)	5"	6+	4+	8	8	N/A	D6	9	2+
	Land Raider (1-4 wounds remaining)	3"	6+	5+	8	8	N/A	D3	9	2+

A Land Raider is equipped with: twin heavy bolter; 2 twin lascannons.

WEAPON	RANGE	TYPE	S	AP	D	ABILITIES
Twin heavy bolter	36"	Heavy 6	5	-1	2	-
Twin lascannon	48"	Heavy 2	9	-3	D6	-

WARGEAR OPTIONS

- This model can be equipped with 1 hunter-killer missile.
- This model can be equipped with 1 storm bolter.
- This model can be equipped with 1 multi-melta.

ABILITIES

Explodes: When this transport is destroyed, roll one D6 before any embarked models disembark and before removing it from play. On a 6 it explodes, and each unit within 6" suffers D6 mortal wounds.

TRANSPORT

This model has a transport capacity of 10 **Grey Knights Infantry** models. Each **Terminator** model takes up the space of 2 models.

FACTION KEYWORDS: **Imperium, Sanctic Astartes, Grey Knights, <Brotherhood>**
KEYWORDS: **Vehicle, Transport, Machine Spirit, Smokescreen, Land Raider**

The Land Raider is a near impregnable transport tank. Large enough to carry Grey Knights wearing Terminator armour, it is yet no mere conveyance. From within armoured housings its Godhammer-pattern lascannons emit deadly spears of power and the roar of its heavy bolters is likened by its crew to the growl of its machine spirit.

LAND RAIDER CRUSADER 15 POWER

Some of this model's characteristics change as it suffers damage, as shown below:

No.	Name	M	WS	BS	S	T	W	A	Ld	Sv
1	Land Raider Crusader (9+ wounds remaining)	10"	6+	3+	8	8	16	6	9	2+
	Land Raider Crusader (5-8 wounds remaining)	5"	6+	4+	8	8	N/A	D6	9	2+
	Land Raider Crusader (1-4 wounds remaining)	3"	6+	5+	8	8	N/A	D3	9	2+

A Land Raider Crusader is equipped with: 2 hurricane bolters; twin assault cannon.

WEAPON	RANGE	TYPE	S	AP	D	ABILITIES
Hurricane bolter	24"	Rapid Fire 6	4	0	1	-
Twin assault cannon	24"	Heavy 12	6	-1	1	-

WARGEAR OPTIONS

- This model can be equipped with 1 hunter-killer missile.
- This model can be equipped with 1 storm bolter.
- This model can be equipped with 1 multi-melta.

ABILITIES

Explodes: When this transport is destroyed, roll one D6 before any embarked models disembark and before removing it from play. On a 6 it explodes, and each unit within 6" suffers D6 mortal wounds.

TRANSPORT

This model has a transport capacity of 16 GREY KNIGHTS INFANTRY models. Each TERMINATOR model takes up the space of 2 models.

FACTION KEYWORDS: IMPERIUM, SANCTIC ASTARTES, GREY KNIGHTS, <BROTHERHOOD>
KEYWORDS: VEHICLE, LAND RAIDER, TRANSPORT, ASSAULT LAUNCHERS, MACHINE SPIRIT, SMOKESCREEN, LAND RAIDER CRUSADER

From its enlarged troop compartment, the Land Raider Crusader delivers a potent cargo of warriors into the presence of the foulest of daemons. All the while, the tank's hurricane bolters and assault cannon tear apart whole swathes of the Chaos Gods' servants.

LAND RAIDER REDEEMER 15 POWER

Some of this model's characteristics change as it suffers damage, as shown below:

No.	Name	M	WS	BS	S	T	W	A	Ld	Sv
1	Land Raider Redeemer (9+ wounds remaining)	10"	6+	3+	8	8	16	6	9	2+
	Land Raider Redeemer (5-8 wounds remaining)	5"	6+	4+	8	8	N/A	D6	9	2+
	Land Raider Redeemer (1-4 wounds remaining)	3"	6+	5+	8	8	N/A	D3	9	2+

A Land Raider Redeemer is equipped with: 2 flamestorm cannons; twin assault cannon.

WEAPON	RANGE	TYPE	S	AP	D	ABILITIES
Flamestorm cannon	12"	Heavy D6	6	-2	2	Each time an attack is made with this weapon, that attack automatically hits the target.
Twin assault cannon	24"	Heavy 12	6	-1	1	-

WARGEAR OPTIONS

- This model can be equipped with 1 hunter-killer missile.
- This model can be equipped with 1 storm bolter.
- This model can be equipped with 1 multi-melta.

ABILITIES

Explodes: When this transport is destroyed, roll one D6 before any embarked models disembark and before removing it from play. On a 6 it explodes, and each unit within 6" suffers D6 mortal wounds.

TRANSPORT

This model has a transport capacity of 12 GREY KNIGHTS INFANTRY models. Each TERMINATOR model takes up the space of 2 models.

FACTION KEYWORDS: IMPERIUM, SANCTIC ASTARTES, GREY KNIGHTS, <BROTHERHOOD>
KEYWORDS: VEHICLE, LAND RAIDER, TRANSPORT, ASSAULT LAUNCHERS, MACHINE SPIRIT, SMOKESCREEN, LAND RAIDER REDEEMER

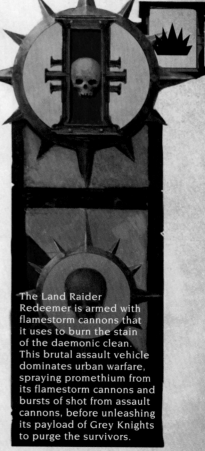

The Land Raider Redeemer is armed with flamestorm cannons that it uses to burn the stain of the daemonic clean. This brutal assault vehicle dominates urban warfare, spraying promethium from its flamestorm cannons and bursts of shot from assault cannons, before unleashing its payload of Grey Knights to purge the survivors.

RAZORBACK

6 POWER

Some of this model's characteristics change as it suffers damage, as shown below:

No.	Name	M	WS	BS	S	T	W	A	Ld	Sv
1	Razorback (6+ wounds remaining)	12"	6+	3+	6	7	10	3	8	3+
	Razorback (3-5 wounds remaining)	6"	6+	4+	6	7	N/A	D3	8	3+
	Razorback (1-2 wounds remaining)	3"	6+	5+	6	7	N/A	1	8	3+

A Razorback is equipped with: twin heavy bolter.

WEAPON	RANGE	TYPE	S	AP	D	ABILITIES
Twin assault cannon	24"	Heavy 12	6	-1	1	-
Twin heavy bolter	36"	Heavy 6	5	-1	2	-
Twin lascannon	48"	Heavy 2	9	-3	D6	-

WARGEAR OPTIONS

- This model's twin heavy bolter can be replaced with one of the following: 1 twin lascannon; 1 twin assault cannon.
- This model can be equipped with 1 hunter-killer missile.
- This model can be equipped with 1 storm bolter.

ABILITIES

Explodes: When this transport is destroyed, roll one D6 before any embarked models disembark and before removing it from play. On a 6 it explodes, and each unit within 6" suffers D3 mortal wounds.

TRANSPORT

This model has a transport capacity of 6 **GREY KNIGHTS INFANTRY** models. It cannot transport **TERMINATOR** models.

FACTION KEYWORDS: IMPERIUM, SANCTIC ASTARTES, GREY KNIGHTS, <BROTHERHOOD>
KEYWORDS: VEHICLE, TRANSPORT, SMOKESCREEN, RAZORBACK

Razorbacks are sturdy armoured transports that combine speed with the support of powerful heavy weapons, ideal for surgical strikes and swift feints. Secure within its adamantine-encased hull, a squad of Grey Knights can advance rapidly and strike exposed foes, while the Razorback's turret engages additional targets.

RHINO

4 POWER

Some of this model's characteristics change as it suffers damage, as shown below:

No.	Name	M	WS	BS	S	T	W	A	Ld	Sv
1	Rhino (6+ wounds remaining)	12"	6+	3+	6	7	10	3	8	3+
	Rhino (3-5 wounds remaining)	6"	6+	4+	6	7	N/A	D3	8	3+
	Rhino (1-2 wounds remaining)	3"	6+	5+	6	7	N/A	1	8	3+

A Rhino is equipped with: storm bolter.

WEAPON	RANGE	TYPE	S	AP	D	ABILITIES
Storm bolter	24"	Rapid Fire 2	4	0	1	-

WARGEAR OPTIONS

- This model can be equipped with 1 hunter-killer missile.
- This model can be equipped with 1 additional storm bolter.

ABILITIES

Explodes: When this transport is destroyed, roll one D6 before any embarked models disembark and before removing it from play. On a 6 it explodes, and each unit within 6" suffers D3 mortal wounds.

TRANSPORT

This model has a transport capacity of 10 **GREY KNIGHTS INFANTRY** models. It cannot transport **TERMINATOR** models.

FACTION KEYWORDS: IMPERIUM, SANCTIC ASTARTES, GREY KNIGHTS, <BROTHERHOOD>
KEYWORDS: VEHICLE, TRANSPORT, SMOKESCREEN, RHINO

The Rhino is an ancient design of transport that has supported Space Marines for millennia. Its rugged and reliable systems are vital for surviving the mutating landscapes of daemon worlds the Grey Knights sometimes fight across, while the warriors inside are shielded by thick armour and a warded truesilver mesh.

STORMHAWK INTERCEPTOR

10 POWER

Some of this model's characteristics change as it suffers damage, as shown below:

No.	Name	M	WS	BS	S	T	W	A	Ld	Sv
1	Stormhawk Interceptor (6+ wounds remaining)	20-60"	6+	3+	6	7	10	3	8	3+
	Stormhawk Interceptor (3-5 wounds remaining)	20-45"	6+	4+	6	7	N/A	D3	8	3+
	Stormhawk Interceptor (1-2 wounds remaining)	20-30"	6+	5+	6	7	N/A	1	8	3+

A Stormhawk Interceptor is equipped with: 2 assault cannons; las-talon; skyhammer missile launcher; infernum halo-launcher.

WEAPON	RANGE	TYPE	S	AP	D	ABILITIES
Assault cannon	24"	Heavy 6	6	-1	1	-
Heavy bolter	36"	Heavy 3	5	-1	2	-
Icarus stormcannon	48"	Heavy 3	7	-1	2	Each time an attack is made with this weapon against an **Aircraft** unit, make 2 hit rolls instead of 1 and add 1 to both those hit rolls.
Las-talon	24"	Heavy 2	9	-3	D6	-
Skyhammer missile launcher	60"	Heavy 3	7	-1	D3	Each time an attack is made with this weapon against an **Aircraft** unit, add 1 to that attack's hit roll.
Typhoon missile launcher	Before selecting targets, select one of the profiles below to make attacks with.					
- Frag missile	48"	Heavy 2D6	4	0	1	Blast
- Krak missile	48"	Heavy 2	8	-2	D6	-

OTHER WARGEAR	ABILITIES
Infernum halo-launcher	Each time a ranged attack made by an **Aircraft** model is allocated to the bearer, add 1 to any armour saving throw made against that attack.

WARGEAR OPTIONS

- This model's skyhammer missile launcher can be replaced with one of the following: 2 heavy bolters; 1 typhoon missile launcher.
- This model's las-talon can be replaced with 1 Icarus stormcannon.

ABILITIES

Airborne: You cannot declare a charge with this model, and it can only be chosen as a target of a charge if the unit making the charge can **Fly**. You can only fight with this model if it is within Engagement Range of any enemy units that can **Fly**, and this model can only make melee attacks against units that can **Fly**. Enemy units can only make melee attacks against this model if they can **Fly**.

Supersonic: Each time this model makes a Normal Move, Advances or Falls Back, first pivot it on the spot up to 90° (this does not contribute to how far the model moves), then move the model straight forwards. It cannot pivot again after the initial pivot.

Hard to Hit: Each time a ranged attack is made against this model, subtract 1 from that attack's hit roll.

Explodes: When this model is destroyed, roll one D6 before removing it from play. On a 6 it explodes, and each unit within 6" suffers D3 mortal wounds.

FACTION KEYWORDS: **Imperium, Sanctic Astartes, Grey Knights, <Brotherhood>**
KEYWORDS: **Vehicle, Aircraft, Fly, Stormhawk Interceptor**

Squadrons of Stormhawk Interceptors – such as the Andaemus Flight – operate at lightning-fast speeds even through warp-tortured skies. Designed to achieve aerial supremacy at high altitudes, the psychic pilots of these aircraft duel not with blades but with batteries of missiles and rapid firing cannons.

STORMTALON GUNSHIP

9 POWER

Some of this model's characteristics change as it suffers damage, as shown below:

No.	Name	M	WS	BS	S	T	W	A	Ld	Sv
1	Stormtalon Gunship (6+ wounds remaining)	20-50"	6+	3+	6	6	10	3	8	3+
	Stormtalon Gunship (3-5 wounds remaining)	20-40"	6+	4+	6	6	N/A	D3	8	3+
	Stormtalon Gunship (1-2 wounds remaining)	20-30"	6+	5+	6	6	N/A	1	8	3+

A Stormtalon Gunship is equipped with: skyhammer missile launcher; twin assault cannon.

WEAPON	RANGE	TYPE	S	AP	D	ABILITIES
Heavy bolter	36"	Heavy 3	5	-1	2	-
Lascannon	48"	Heavy 1	9	-3	D6	-
Skyhammer missile launcher	60"	Heavy 3	7	-1	D3	Each time an attack is made with this weapon against an **AIRCRAFT** unit, add 1 to that attack's hit roll.
Twin assault cannon	24"	Heavy 12	6	-1	1	-
Typhoon missile launcher	Before selecting targets, select one of the profiles below to make attacks with.					
- Frag missile	48"	Heavy 2D6	4	0	1	Blast
- Krak missile	48"	Heavy 2	8	-2	D6	-

WARGEAR OPTIONS

- This model's skyhammer missile launcher can be replaced with one of the following: 2 heavy bolters; 2 lascannons; 1 typhoon missile launcher.

ABILITIES

Airborne: You cannot declare a charge with this model, and it can only be chosen as a target of a charge if the unit making the charge can **FLY**. You can only fight with this model if it is within Engagement Range of any enemy units that can **FLY**, and this model can only make melee attacks against units that can **FLY**. Enemy units can only make melee attacks against this model if they can **FLY**.

Supersonic: Each time this model makes a Normal Move, Advances or Falls Back, first pivot it on the spot up to 90° (this does not contribute to how far the model moves), then move the model straight forwards. It cannot pivot again after the initial pivot.

Hard to Hit: Each time a ranged attack is made against this model, subtract 1 from that attack's hit roll.

Hover Jet: In your Command phase, this model can hover. If it does, then until the start of your next Command phase, its Move characteristic becomes 20" and it loses the Airborne, Hard to Hit and Supersonic abilities.

Explodes: When this model is destroyed, roll one D6 before removing it from play. On a 6 it explodes, and each unit within 6" suffers D3 mortal wounds.

FACTION KEYWORDS: IMPERIUM, SANCTIC ASTARTES, GREY KNIGHTS, <BROTHERHOOD>
KEYWORDS: VEHICLE, AIRCRAFT, FLY, STORMTALON GUNSHIP

Stormtalon Gunships are highly manoeuvrable aircraft as versatile in role as in their choice of target. Often running escort duties for larger craft, they hunt down enemy fighters or terrifying warp-spawned drakes. Using vectored afterburners, their pilots unleash ground attacks, saturating teleportation zones with fire and clearing them for their brothers.

STORMRAVEN GUNSHIP

17 POWER

Some of this model's characteristics change as it suffers damage, as shown below:

No.	Name	M	WS	BS	S	T	W	A	Ld	Sv
1	Stormraven Gunship (8+wounds remaining)	20-45"	6+	3+	8	7	14	6	9	3+
	Stormraven Gunship (4-7 wounds remaining)	20-35"	6+	4+	8	7	N/A	D6	9	3+
	Stormraven Gunship (1-3 wounds remaining)	20-25"	6+	5+	8	7	N/A	D3	9	3+

A Stormraven Gunship is equipped with: 2 stormstrike missile launchers; twin assault cannon; typhoon missile launcher.

WEAPON	RANGE	TYPE	S	AP	D	ABILITIES
Hurricane bolter	24"	Rapid Fire 6	4	0	1	-
Stormstrike missile launcher	72"	Heavy 1	8	-3	3	-
Twin assault cannon	24"	Heavy 12	6	-1	1	-
Twin heavy bolter	36"	Heavy 6	5	-1	2	-
Twin heavy plasma cannon	Before selecting targets, select one of the profiles below to make attacks with.					
- Standard	36"	Heavy 2D3	7	-3	2	Blast
- Supercharge	36"	Heavy 2D3	8	-3	3	Blast. Each time an unmodified hit roll of 1 is made for an attack with this weapon profile, the bearer suffers 1 mortal wound after shooting with this weapon.
Twin lascannon	48"	Heavy 2	9	-3	D6	-
Twin multi-melta	24"	Heavy 4	8	-4	D6	Each time an attack made with this weapon targets a unit within half range, that attack has a Damage characteristic of D6+2.
Typhoon missile launcher	Before selecting targets, select one of the profiles below to make attacks with.					
- Frag missile	48"	Heavy 2D6	4	0	1	Blast
- Krak missile	48"	Heavy 2	8	-2	D6	-

WARGEAR OPTIONS

- This model's twin assault cannon can be replaced with one of the following: 1 twin heavy plasma cannon; 1 twin lascannon.
- This model's typhoon missile launcher can be replaced with one of the following: 1 twin heavy bolter; 1 twin multi-melta.
- This model can be equipped with 2 hurricane bolters.

ABILITIES

Airborne: You cannot declare a charge with this model, and it can only be chosen as a target of a charge if the unit making the charge can **FLY**. You can only fight with this model if it is within Engagement Range of any enemy units that can **FLY**, and this model can only make melee attacks against units that can **FLY**. Enemy units can only make melee attacks against this model if they can **FLY**.

Supersonic: Each time this model makes a Normal Move, Advances or Falls Back, first pivot it on the spot up to 90° (this does not contribute to how far the model moves), then move the model straight forwards. It cannot pivot again after the initial pivot.

Hard to Hit: Each time a ranged attack is made against this model, subtract 1 from that attack's hit roll.

Hover Jet: In your Command phase, this model can hover. If it does, then until the start of your next Command phase, its Move characteristic becomes 20" and it loses the Airborne, Hard to Hit and Supersonic abilities.

Explodes: When this transport is destroyed, roll one D6 before any embarked models disembark and before removing it from play. On a 6 it explodes, and each unit within 6" suffers D6 mortal wounds.

TRANSPORT

This model has a transport capacity of 12 GREY KNIGHTS INFANTRY models and 1 GREY KNIGHTS DREADNOUGHT model. Each TERMINATOR model takes the space of two INFANTRY models.

FACTION KEYWORDS: **IMPERIUM, SANCTIC ASTARTES, GREY KNIGHTS, <BROTHERHOOD>**
KEYWORDS: **VEHICLE, AIRCRAFT, TRANSPORT, FLY, MACHINE SPIRIT, STORMRAVEN GUNSHIP**

Powerful close-support aircraft, Stormraven Gunships are capable of deploying Grey Knights and even a revered Dreadnought where empyric disturbances prevent teleportation. Resilient and bristling with heavy weapons, Stormravens excel in armoured assaults and the fiery purgations of landing zones.

WEAPON PROFILES

On pages 105-106 you will find the profiles for all the weapons that Grey Knights models can be equipped with. Note that some weapons have the Blast ability; this ability is detailed in full in the Warhammer 40,000 Core Book.

WEAPON LISTS

The wargear options section of some datasheets in this Codex refer to one or more weapon lists. These lists can be found below:

COMBI-WEAPONS
- Combi-flamer
- Combi-melta
- Combi-plasma

MELEE WEAPONS
- Nemesis daemon hammer
- Nemesis force halberd
- Nemesis force sword
- Nemesis warding stave
- Two Nemesis falchions

SPECIAL WEAPONS
- Incinerator
- Psilencer
- Psycannon

WEAPON DEFINITIONS

Some rules refer to 'bolt weapons', 'flame weapons', 'nemesis weapons' or 'psi weapons'. The definitions of these weapons for the purposes of such rules can be found below:

Bolt Weapons
A bolt weapon is any ranged weapon whose profile includes the word 'bolt' (storm bolter, master-crafted storm bolter, twin heavy bolter etc.), and any Relic that replaces a bolt weapon (e.g. Fury of Deimos, page 62). Rules that apply to bolt weapons only apply to the boltgun profile of combi-weapons, and the boltgun profile of Relics that replace combi-weapons. If a bolt weapon has a shooting and melee profile, rules that apply to bolt weapons only apply to the shooting profile of that weapon.

Flame Weapons
A flame weapon is any ranged weapon whose profile includes the word 'flame' (flamer, flamestorm cannon, heavy flamer etc.) or 'incinerator' (incinerator, heavy incinerator etc), as well as any Relic that replaces a flame weapon. Rules that apply to flame weapons only apply to the flamer profile of combi-flamers, and the flamer profile of Relics that replace combi-flamers. If a flame weapon has a shooting and melee profile, rules that apply to flame weapons only apply to the shooting profile of that weapon.

Nemesis Weapons
A Nemesis weapon is any melee weapon whose profile includes the word 'Nemesis' (Nemesis force halberd, Nemesis daemon hammer, Nemesis greatsword etc.), and any Relic that replaces a Nemesis weapon. Note that the following weapons found in this Codex are also Nemesis weapons:

- Malleus Argyrum
- The Titansword

Psi Weapons
A psi weapon is any ranged weapon whose profile includes the word 'psy' or 'psi' (psilencer, psycannon, gatling psilencer etc.), and any Relic that replaces a psi weapon.

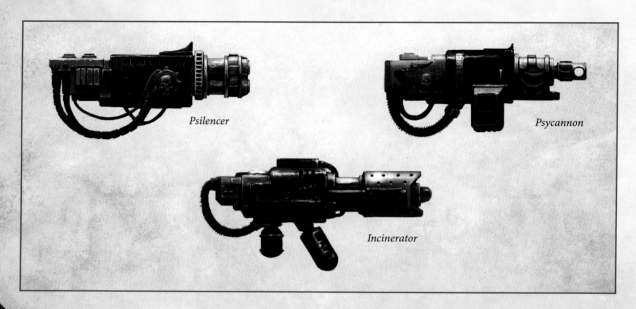

Psilencer

Psycannon

Incinerator

RANGED WEAPONS	RANGE	TYPE	S	AP	D	ABILITIES
Assault cannon	24"	Heavy 6	6	-1	1	-
Bolt pistol	12"	Pistol 1	4	0	1	-
Boltgun	24"	Rapid Fire 1	4	0	1	-
Combi-flamer		Before selecting targets, select one or both of the profiles below to make attacks with. If you select both, then each time an attack is made with this weapon this phase, subtract 1 from that attack's hit roll.				
- Boltgun	24"	Rapid Fire 1	4	0	1	-
- Flamer	12"	Assault D6	4	0	1	Each time an attack is made with this weapon profile, that attack automatically hits the target.
Combi-melta		Before selecting targets, select one or both of the profiles below to make attacks with. If you select both, then each time an attack is made with this weapon this phase, subtract 1 from that attack's hit roll.				
- Boltgun	24"	Rapid Fire 1	4	0	1	-
- Meltagun	12"	Assault 1	8	-4	D6	Each time an attack made with this weapon profile targets a unit within half range, that attack has a Damage characteristic of D6+2.
Combi-plasma		Before selecting targets, select one or two of the profiles below to make attacks with (you can only select one of the plasma gun profiles). If you select two, then each time an attack is made with this weapon this phase, subtract 1 from that attack's hit roll.				
- Boltgun	24"	Rapid Fire 1	4	0	1	-
- Plasma (standard)	24"	Rapid Fire 1	7	-3	1	-
- Plasma (supercharge)	24"	Rapid Fire 1	8	-3	2	If any unmodified hit rolls of 1 are made for attacks with this weapon profile, the bearer is destroyed after shooting with this weapon.
Flamer	12"	Assault D6	4	0	1	Each time an attack is made with this weapon, that attack automatically hits the target.
Flamestorm cannon	12"	Heavy D6	6	-2	2	Each time an attack is made with this weapon, that attack automatically hits the target.
Frag grenades	6"	Grenade D6	3	0	1	Blast
Gatling psilencer	24"	Heavy 12	5	-1	1	-
Heavy bolter	36"	Heavy 3	5	-1	2	-
Heavy flamer	12"	Heavy D6	5	-1	1	Each time an attack is made with this weapon, that attack automatically hits the target
Heavy incinerator	12"	Heavy 2D6	6	-1	1	Each time an attack is made with this weapon, that attack automatically hits the target.
Heavy plasma cannon		Before selecting targets, select one of the profiles below to make attacks with.				
- Standard	36"	Heavy D3	7	-3	2	Blast
- Supercharge	36"	Heavy D3	8	-3	3	Blast. Each time an unmodified hit roll of 1 is made for an attack with this weapon profile, the bearer suffers 1 mortal wound after shooting with this weapon.
Heavy psycannon	24"	Heavy 6	8	-2	2	-
Hunter-killer missile	48"	Heavy 1	10	-2	D6	The bearer can only shoot with each hunter-killer missile it is equipped with once per battle.
Hurricane bolter	24"	Rapid Fire 6	4	0	1	-
Icarus stormcannon	48"	Heavy 3	7	-1	2	Each time an attack is made with this weapon against an AIRCRAFT unit, make 2 hit rolls instead of 1 and add 1 to both those hit rolls.
Incinerator	12"	Heavy D6	6	-1	1	Each time an attack is made with this weapon, that attack automatically hits the target
Krak grenades	6"	Grenade 1	6	-1	D3	-
Lascannon	48"	Heavy 1	9	-3	D6	-
Las-talon	24"	Heavy 2	9	-3	D6	-
Missile launcher		Before selecting targets, select one of the profiles below to make attacks with.				
- Frag missile	48"	Heavy D6	4	0	1	Blast
- Krak missile	48"	Heavy 1	8	-2	D6	-
Master-crafted storm bolter	24"	Rapid Fire 2	4	-1	2	-
Multi-melta	24"	Heavy 2	8	-4	D6	Each time an attack made with this weapon targets a unit within half range, that attack has a Damage characteristic of D6+2.
Plasma cannon		Before selecting targets, select one of the profiles below to make attacks with.				
- Standard	36"	Heavy D3	7	-3	1	Blast
- Supercharge	36"	Heavy D3	8	-3	2	Blast. If any unmodified hit rolls of 1 are made for attacks with this weapon profile, the bearer is destroyed after shooting with this weapon.
Plasma cutter		Before selecting targets, select one of the profiles below to make attacks with.				
- Standard	12"	Assault 1	7	-3	1	-
- Supercharge	12"	Assault 1	8	-3	2	If any unmodified hit rolls of 1 are made for attacks with this weapon profile, the bearer is destroyed after shooting with this weapon.

RANGED WEAPONS	RANGE	TYPE	S	AP	D	ABILITIES
Psilencer	24"	Heavy 6	4	-1	1	-
Psycannon	24"	Heavy 3	7	-1	2	-
Skyhammer missile launcher	60"	Heavy 3	7	-1	D3	Each time an attack is made with this weapon against an **AIRCRAFT** unit, add 1 to that attack's hit roll.
Storm bolter	24"	Rapid Fire 2	4	0	1	-
Stormstrike missile launcher	72"	Heavy 1	8	-3	3	-
Twin assault cannon	24"	Heavy 12	6	-1	1	-
Twin heavy bolter	36"	Heavy 6	5	-1	2	-
Twin heavy plasma cannon	Before selecting targets, select one of the profiles below to make attacks with.					
- Standard	36"	Heavy 2D3	7	-3	2	Blast
- Supercharge	36"	Heavy 2D3	8	-3	3	Blast. Each time an unmodified hit roll of 1 is made for an attack with this weapon profile, the bearer suffers 1 mortal wound after shooting with this weapon.
Twin lascannon	48"	Heavy 2	9	-3	D6	-
Twin multi-melta	24"	Heavy 4	8	-4	D6	Each time an attack made with this weapon targets a unit within half range, that attack has a Damage characteristic of D6+2.
Typhoon missile launcher	Before selecting targets, select one of the profiles below to make attacks with.					
- Frag missile	48"	Heavy 2D6	4	0	1	Blast
- Krak missile	48"	Heavy 2	8	-2	D6	-

MELEE WEAPONS	RANGE	TYPE	S	AP	D	ABILITIES
Black Blade of Antwyr	Melee	Melee	+1	-3	2	Each time an attack is made with this weapon, an unmodified wound roll of 6 inflicts D3 mortal wounds on the target in addition to any normal damage.
Crozius arcanum	Melee	Melee	+2	-1	2	-
Dreadfist	Melee	Melee	x2	-3	2	-
Dreadnought close combat weapon	Melee	Melee	x2	-3	3	-
Malleus Argyrum	Melee	Melee	x2	-3	3	-
Nemesis daemon greathammer	Melee	Melee	x2	-4	D3+3	Each time an attack is made with this weapon, subtract 1 from that attack's hit roll.
Nemesis daemon hammer	Melee	Melee	x2	-2	3	Each time an attack is made with this weapon, subtract 1 from that attack's hit roll.
Nemesis falchion	Melee	Melee	User	-2	1	Each time the bearer fights, if it is equipped with one or more Nemesis falchions, it makes 1 additional attack using this profile.
Nemesis force halberd	Melee	Melee	+2	-2	2	-
Nemesis force sword	Melee	Melee	+1	-3	2	-
Nemesis greatsword	Before selecting targets, select one of the profiles below to make attacks with.					
- Mighty strike	Melee	Melee	+4	-3	D6	-
- Sweeping blow	Melee	Melee	User	-2	2	Make 2 hit rolls for each attack made with this profile, instead of 1.
Nemesis warding stave	Melee	Melee	+3	-1	2	-
Omnissian power axe	Melee	Melee	+2	-2	2	-
Servo-arm	Melee	Melee	x2	-2	3	Each time the bearer fights, no more than one attack can be made with each servo-arm.
The Titansword	Melee	Melee	+4	-4	3	-

Nemesis warding stave

Nemesis daemon hammer

Nemesis force halberd

Nemesis falchions

Frag grenade

Psyk-out grenade

Nemesis force sword

WARGEAR

107

POINTS VALUES

You can use this section to determine the points (pts) value of each unit in your army. Each entry lists the unit's size (i.e. how many models the unit can contain) and how many points the unit costs. If an entry has a unit cost of 'x pts/model', then the unit costs x points for every model in that unit. You must then add points for each weapon, or item of wargear, that is included in that unit if it is listed in that unit's entry (weapons and wargear not listed in a unit's entry cost no additional points to include in that unit).

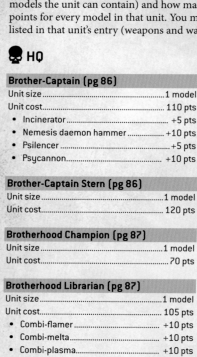

💀 HQ

Brother-Captain (pg 86)
Unit size .... 1 model
Unit cost .... 110 pts
- Incinerator .... +5 pts
- Nemesis daemon hammer .... +10 pts
- Psilencer .... +5 pts
- Psycannon .... +10 pts

Brother-Captain Stern (pg 86)
Unit size .... 1 model
Unit cost .... 120 pts

Brotherhood Champion (pg 87)
Unit size .... 1 model
Unit cost .... 70 pts

Brotherhood Librarian (pg 87)
Unit size .... 1 model
Unit cost .... 105 pts
- Combi-flamer .... +10 pts
- Combi-melta .... +10 pts
- Combi-plasma .... +10 pts
- Nemesis daemon hammer .... +10 pts
- Storm bolter .... +5 pts

Brotherhood Techmarine (pg 88)
Unit size .... 1 model
Unit cost .... 80 pts

Castellan Crowe (pg 85)
Unit size .... 1 model
Unit cost .... 90 pts

Grand Master (pg 83)
Unit size .... 1 model
Unit cost .... 135 pts
- Incinerator .... +5 pts
- Nemesis daemon hammer .... +10 pts
- Psilencer .... +5 pts
- Psycannon .... +10 pts

Grand Master in Nemesis Dreadknight (pg 84)
Unit size .... 1 model
Unit cost .... 150 pts
- Dreadknight Teleporter .... +10 pts
- Gatling Psilencer .... +20 pts
- Heavy incinerator .... +15 pts
- Heavy psycannon .... +20 pts
- Nemesis daemon greathammer .... +10 pts
- Nemesis greatsword .... +15 pts

Grand Master Voldus (pg 83)
Unit size .... 1 model
Unit cost .... 150 pts

Brotherhood Chaplain (pg 89)
Unit size .... 1 model
Unit cost .... 110 pts

Kaldor Draigo (pg 82)
Unit size .... 1 model
Unit cost .... 180 pts

▶ TROOPS

Brotherhood Terminator Squad (pg 89)
Unit size .... 5-10 models
Unit cost .... 42 pts/model
- Incinerator .... +5 pts
- Nemesis daemon hammer .... +10 pts
- Psilencer .... +5 pts
- Psycannon .... +10 pts

Strike Squad (pg 90)
Unit size .... 5-10 models
Unit cost .... 22 pts/model
- Nemesis daemon hammer .... +10 pts
- Psycannon .... +5 pts

☠ ELITES

Brotherhood Apothecary (pg 91)
Unit size .... 1 model
Unit cost .... 100 pts
- Nemesis daemon hammer .... +10 pts

Brotherhood Ancient (pg 91)
Unit size .... 1 model
Unit cost .... 100 pts
- Nemesis falchion .... +5 pts

Dreadnought (pg 95)
Unit size .... 1 model
Unit cost .... 130 pts
- Heavy flamer .... +10 pts
- Multi-melta .... +5 pts
- Twin lascannon .... +20 pts

Paladin Ancient (pg 93)
Unit size .... 1 model
Unit cost .... 110 pts
- Incinerator .... +5 pts
- Nemesis falchion .... +5 pts
- Psilencer .... +10 pts
- Psycannon .... +10 pts

Paladin Squad (pg 92)
Unit size .... 3-10 models
Unit cost .... 47 pts/model
- Incinerator .... +5 pts
- Nemesis daemon hammer .... +10 pts
- Psilencer .... +5 pts
- Psycannon .... +10 pts

Purifier Squad (pg 92)
Unit size .... 5-10 models
Unit cost .... 23 pts/model
- Nemesis daemon hammer .... +10 pts
- Psycannon .... +5 pts

Servitors (pg 93)
Unit size .... 4 models
Unit cost .... 30 pts
- Heavy bolter .... +5 pts
- Multi-melta .... +10 pts
- Plasma cannon .... +5 pts

Venerable Dreadnought (pg 94)
Unit size .... 1 model
Unit cost .... 145 pts
- Heavy flamer .... +10 pts
- Multi-melta .... +5 pts
- Twin lascannon .... +20 pts

⚡ FAST ATTACK

Interceptor Squad (pg 96)
Unit size .... 5-10 models
Unit cost .... 24 pts/model
- Nemesis daemon hammer .... +10 pts
- Psycannon .... +5 pts

♛ HEAVY SUPPORT

Land Raider (pg 98)
Unit size ....1 model
Unit cost... 285 pts
- Hunter-killer missile .... +5 pts
- Multi-melta .... +25 pts
- Storm bolter.....................................+5 pts

Land Raider Crusader (pg 99)
Unit size ....1 model
Unit cost... 285 pts
- Hunter-killer missile .... +5 pts
- Multi-melta .... +25 pts
- Storm bolter.....................................+5 pts

Land Raider Redeemer (pg 99)
Unit size ....1 model
Unit cost... 285 pts
- Hunter-killer missile .... +5 pts
- Multi-melta .... +25 pts
- Storm bolter.....................................+5 pts

Nemesis Dreadknight (pg 97)
Unit size ....1 model
Unit cost... 120 pts
- Dreadknight Teleporter........................ +10 pts
- Gatling Psilencer .... +20 pts
- Heavy incinerator .... +15 pts
- Heavy psycannon .... +20 pts
- Nemesis daemon greathammer .... +10 pts
- Nemesis greatsword............................ +15 pts

Purgation Squad (pg 96)
Unit size .... 5-10 models
Unit cost..22 pts/model
- Nemesis daemon hammer .... +10 pts
- Psycannon.. +5 pts

☗ DEDICATED TRANSPORTS

Razorback (pg 100)
Unit size ....1 model
Unit cost...................................... 110 pts/model
- Hunter-killer missile .... +5 pts
- Storm bolter....................................... +5 pts
- Twin assault cannon .... +15 pts
- Twin lascannon...................................... +10 pts

Rhino (pg 100)
Unit size ....1 model
Unit cost..80 pts/model
- Additional storm bolter............................+5 pts
- Hunter-killer missile .... +5 pts

❦❦ FLYERS

Stormhawk Interceptor (pg 101)
Unit size ....1 model
Unit cost... 185 pts
- Heavy bolter... +5 pts
- Las-talon .... +25 pts
- Typhoon missile launcher................... +20 pts

Stormraven Gunship (pg 103)
Unit size ....1 model
Unit cost... 310 pts
- Hurricane bolter .... +15 pts
- Twin assault cannon .... +10 pts
- Twin lascannon...................................... +10 pts
- Twin Multi-melta .... +20 pts
- Typhoon missile launcher................... +10 pts

Stormtalon Gunship (pg 102)
Unit size ....1 model
Unit cost... 165 pts
- Heavy bolter... +5 pts
- Lascannon.. +10 pts
- Typhoon missile launcher................... +20 pts

WISDOM OF THE PROGNOSTICARS

Visions of the Augurium (pg 55)
- Augury of Aggression.. +20 pts
- Heroism's Favour .... +15 pts
- A Noble Death .... +20 pts
- Omen of Incursion .... +30 pts
- Presaged Paralysis... +15 pts
- Foretelling of Locus.. +30 pts

Gifts of the Prescient (pg 56)
- True Name Shard.. +10 pts
- Temporal Bombs .... +15 pts
- Servant of the Throne .... +20 pts
- Deluminator of Majesty... +15 pts
- Gem of Inoktu.. +15 pts
- Severance Bolt .... +30 pts

GLOSSARY

On this page you will find a glossary that contains a number of terms used in this Codex. These are intended to provide precise definitions to help resolve some of the more complex rules interactions that may arise, and players should feel under no obligation to memorise this list.

The Aegis: A bonus available to GREY KNIGHTS PSYKER units in a GREY KNIGHTS Detachment.

Any number of models can each have their *Weapon A* replaced with 1 *Weapon B*: When this wargear option is selected for a unit, any number of models in that unit that are equipped with Weapon A can each have its weapon replaced Weapon B. It is possible for only some of the models in that unit to have their weapon replaced and for others not to.

Bolt weapon: A ranged weapon whose profile includes the word 'bolt', or a Relic that replaces a bolt weapon. The boltgun profile of a combi-weapon is also a bolt weapon, as are any of the weapons listed under Bolt Weapons on page 104.

Brotherhood: GREY KNIGHTS units with the <BROTHERHOOD> keyword will belong to one of the eight brotherhoods. When you include such a unit in your army you must select which of these to replace this keyword with: Swordbearers; Blades of Victory; Wardmakers; Prescient Brethren; Preservers; Rapiers; Exactors; Silver Blades.

Brotherhood of Psykers Detachment (pg 45): A GREY KNIGHTS Detachment in which every unit (excluding AGENT OF THE IMPERIUM, UNALIGNED and HONOURED KNIGHT units) is drawn from the same brotherhood.

Brotherhood psychic power (pg 46-53): A psychic power associated with one of the eight brotherhoods. These are only known by PSYKER units that are part of a Brotherhood of Psykers Detachment (and only if they are drawn from the associated brotherhood).

Brotherhood Stratagem (pg 46-53): A Stratagem associated with one of the eight brotherhoods. If your army includes a Brotherhood of Psykers Detachment (excluding Auxiliary Support, Super-heavy Auxiliary and Fortification Network Detachments), then you will gain access to the associated brotherhood Stratagem.

Brotherhood Warlord Trait (pg 46-53): A Warlord Trait associated with one of the eight brotherhoods. These are only available to WARLORDS that are part of a Brotherhood of Psykers Detachment (and only if they are drawn from the associated brotherhood).

Dominant Tide: The Tide of the Warp that is currently dominant, as part of the Masters of the Warp ability (pg 81).

Daemonic Nemesis (pg 77): An additional set of rules that can apply during Crusade battles that include any GREY KNIGHTS CHARACTER units.

Flame weapon: A ranged weapon whose profile includes the word 'flame' or 'incinerator', or a Relic that replaces one of these weapons. The flamer profile of a combi-flamer is also a flame weapon.

Gift: Shorthand for Gift of the Prescient (see opposite).

Gift of the Prescient: One of the two types of Wisdom of the Prognosticars (pg 56).

GREY KNIGHTS Detachment (pg 45): A Detachment in a Battle-forged army where every model has the GREY KNIGHTS keyword (excluding models with the AGENT OF THE IMPERIUM or UNALIGNED keywords).

GREY KNIGHTS secondary objectives (pg 68): Additional secondary objectives that can be used in certain matched play mission packs if every Detachment in your army is a GREY KNIGHTS Detachment.

Honoured Titles (pg 73): A Crusade Battle Honour category that can only be taken by GRAND MASTER units.

Litany: A Litany of Purity. GREY KNIGHTS PRIEST models can attempt to recite litanies that they know.

Maximum number of models: A unit contains the maximum number of models if it includes every model it possibly can, as described on its datasheet.

Nemesis weapon: A melee weapon whose profile includes the word 'Nemesis', or a Relic that replaces a Nemesis weapon. The Titansword and Malleus Argyrum are also Nemesis weapons.

Psi weapon: A ranged weapon whose profile includes the word 'psi' or 'psy', or a Relic that replaces such a weapon.

Psychic power type: A psychic power's type is written in **bold** at the start of its rules. There are three types of psychic power described in this Codex: Blessing; Malediction; Witchfire.

Relic of Titan: A type of Relic that can be given to GREY KNIGHTS CHARACTER models.

Stratagem label: A Stratagem's labels are written beneath its title and can include: Grey Knights; Battle Tactic; Epic Deed, Strategic Ploy; Requisition; Wargear. A Stratagem can have more than one label; for example, a Stratagem with 'Grey Knights – Wargear Stratagem' has both the Grey Knights and Wargear labels.

Vision: Shorthand for Vision of the Augurium (see below).

Vision of the Augurium: One of the two types of Wisdom of the Prognosticars (pg 55).

Wisdom of the Prognosticars (pg 54-56): An upgrade that can be applied to GREY KNIGHTS CHARACTER models (excluding named characters). There are two types of Wisdom of Prognosticars: Visions of the Augurium and Gifts of the Prescient.

RULES REFERENCE

REFERENCE

Below you will find a bullet-pointed summary of several Grey Knights rules. In most games, you may find referencing this summary is all you need to resolve a rule, but if not, follow the page reference to read the entirety of the rule.

THE AEGIS (PG 45)

- Each time a model with this ability would lose a wound as a result of a mortal wound, roll one D6: on a 5+, that wound is not lost.
- If a PSYKER unit has this ability, add 1 to Deny the Witch tests taken for that unit.

AND THEY SHALL KNOW NO FEAR (PG 80)

- Ignore modifiers when taking Combat Attrition tests.

BOLTER DISCIPLINE (PG 80)

- Make double the number of attacks when shooting a Rapid Fire bolt weapon if the target is within half range, or if the shooting model is an INFANTRY model whose unit Remained Stationary in its previous Movement phase, or if the shooting model is a TERMINATOR model.

<BROTHERHOOD> KEYWORD (PG 80)

- When you include a unit with the <BROTHERHOOD> keyword, nominate which brotherhood it is drawn from.
- Replace every instance of the <BROTHERHOOD> keyword on that unit's datasheet with the name of your chosen brotherhood.

COMBAT SQUADS (PG 80)

- If unit contains maximum number of models, it can be split into two units at the start of deployment, containing as equal a number of models as possible.

BROTHERHOOD COMMAND (PG 45)

- Can include a maximum of one GRAND MASTER and one BROTHER-CAPTAIN model in each Detachment.
- Each GRAND MASTER in your army must be from a different brotherhood.
- Each BROTHER-CAPTAIN in your army must be from a different brotherhood.

BROTHERHOOD OF PSYKERS (PG 45)

- If your army is Battle-forged, <BROTHERHOOD> GREY KNIGHTS Detachments in your army gain access to Warlord Traits, psychic powers and Stratagems provided every model in that Detachment that is drawn from a brotherhood is from the same brotherhood.

DETACHMENT ABILITIES (PG 45)

- If army Battle-forged, GREY KNIGHTS Detachments gain the Brotherhood Command ability.
- If army Battle-forged, GREY KNIGHTS units in GREY KNIGHTS Detachments gain The Aegis ability.
- If army Battle-forged, GREY KNIGHTS Troops units in GREY KNIGHTS Detachments gain objective secured ability (see Warhammer 40,000 Core Book).
- Does not apply to Auxiliary Support, Super-heavy Auxiliary and Fortification Network Detachments.

HONOURED TITLES (PG 73)

- GRAND MASTERS can have a single Honoured Title instead of gaining a Battle Trait.
- Increases model's Crusade points by 1.
- Cannot have two GRAND MASTERS in your Order of Battle with the same Honoured Title.

KNIGHTS OF TITAN (PG 80)

- Unit has the following abilities: And They Shall Know No Fear, Bolter Discipline, Masters of the Warp.

PSYCHIC CONFLUENCE (PG 65)

- Can attempt to manifest psychic powers from the Sanctic Discipline even if they have already been manifested this phase.
- Add 1 to warp charge value of these psychic powers for each other attempt that has been made to manifest them during the same phase, whether successful or not.

MASTERS OF THE WARP (PG 81)

- Masters of the Warp applies if every model in your army has the GREY KNIGHTS keyword (excluding AGENT OF THE IMPERIUM and UNALIGNED models).
- At start of battle, choose which Tide is dominant.
- Can change which Tide is dominant for your army by successfully manifesting the *Warp Shaping* psychic power.
- **Tide of Banishment:** Unit gains following aura ability: 'Subtract 2 from the Leadership characteristic of enemy DAEMON units while they are within 6" of

this unit'. In addition, each time a model in this unit makes an attack against a DAEMON unit, re-roll hit rolls of 1 and re-roll wound rolls of 1.
- **Tide of Celerity:** Each time this unit Advances or charges, treat each individual dice roll of 1-2 as 3 instead.
- **Tide of Convergence:** Add 6" to the range of all psi weapons that models in the unit are equipped with. Each time a model in this unit attacks with a Nemesis weapon, on an unmodified wound roll of 6, the target suffers 1 mortal wound in addition to any normal damage.
- **Tide of Escalation:** Unit can attempt to manifest brotherhood psychic powers even if they have already been manifested this phase. Add 1 to warp charge value of these psychic powers for each other attempt that has been made to manifest them during the same phase, whether successful or not.
- **Tide of Shadows:** Unit counts as receiving Light Cover against ranged attacks made from more than 12" away. If unit already receives Light Cover, they additionally receive Dense Cover.

TELEPORT STRIKE (PG 80)

- During deployment, can set unit up in a teleportarium chamber instead of setting them up on the battlefield.
- Unit can then arrive during Reinforcements step of one of your Movement phases.
- When unit arrives, set it up on battlefield more than 9" from any enemy models.

WISDOM OF THE PROGNOSTICARS (PG 54-56)

- If Battle-forged, can upgrade GREY KNIGHTS CHARACTER models.
- Doing so increases model's Power Rating and points value.
- Upgraded character will gain either a Vision of the Augurium or a Gift of the Prescient.
- Army cannot contain more than one model with the same Vision or Gift.
- Crusade armies must use Consult the Prognosticars Requisition to upgrade characters.
- Cannot upgrade named characters.